Naturally Sweet
Vegan Treats

Plant-Based Delights Free from
Refined and Artificial Sweeteners

Marisa Alvarsson

Creator of Miss Marzipan

PAGE STREET
PUBLISHING CO.

PAGE STREET
PUBLISHING CO.

Distributed by Macmillan, sales in Canada by The Canadian Manda Group.

22   21   20   19   18   1   2   3   4   5

ISBN-13: 978-1-62414-609-1
ISBN-10: 1-62414-609-0

Library of Congress Control Number: 2018932224

Cover and book design by Rosie Stewart for Page Street Publishing Co.
Photography by Marisa Alvarsson

Printed and bound in China

This book is dedicated to my children and my husband
who remind me to celebrate "the every day" every day,
to everyone who has supported me, and to all who aspire
to live well, love wholeheartedly and shine brightly.

Table of Contents

Introduction

Hello!

Thank you for picking up this book about enjoyment—enjoyment of the sweet things in life: time with loved ones, time for yourself, food, fun and, you guessed it, treats. And yes, they're vegan and naturally sweetened, as the title suggests. But this isn't a book about restrictions, limitations, dos and don'ts; it's about alternatives.

When we discovered my daughter's severe infant dairy protein intolerance in 2013 and my husband decided to become an ethical vegan overnight, I was catapulted into learning about dairy- and egg-free baking, whilst making use of the things we had access to. I started my own sugar-reducing journey (both the obvious and hidden varieties) in 2014, which I documented on my Miss Marzipan blog, and, somewhat ironically, I returned to the classroom to earn my pastry diploma here in Stockholm that same year. I learned some wonderful traditional pastry techniques, and it was both fun and fascinating. However, to be honest, little of what I learned was directly convertible to the making of vegan treats, let alone vegan and white-sugar-free ones! I have had to rely heavily on experimentation over the years, in conjunction with taking on feedback from my toughest critics in the form of 1-, 4- and 6-year-olds!

Though the recipes in this book are not entirely sugar-free because all fruit, unrefined sweeteners and even vegetables contain natural sugars, they are naturally sweetened with refined sugar alternatives that are plant-derived and vegan.

If you're new to plant-based baking or low-sugar eating, or someone in your family has thrown a dietary curve ball into the meal prep field, I feel you! The good news is that it does make for an interesting culinary adventure and, I have found, a rewarding one. Today, the very treats in this book are the ones I make with my kids and those I serve to my family and friends.

We live in Sweden, where something known as fika (pronounced fee-ka) is a near sacrosanct social institution. Fika—both a noun and a verb—describes pausing in the day to savor a cup of coffee, tea or a cold beverage accompanied by something sweet. This takes place most often in the mid-morning or mid-afternoon—and sometimes both. Perhaps it's because I am immersed in fika culture that I really am not opposed to its enjoyment on a fairly regular basis. To me, fika isn't merely about consumption of caffeine or sweet things. It's a way to be mindfully cozy, as opposed to grabbing a cup of coffee-to-go and drinking it as you race from one place to the next. I find that simply taking the time to pause and enjoy a break is a way to increase the happiness quotient in my day. On the other hand, overconsumption of sugar, particularly refined sugar, does not make me happy. My body simply does not respond well to it.

I am not anti-sugar, but I've had to be mindful about its overconsumption for quite some time on account of my medical history. And so, without labeling ourselves sugar-free, my family is what I describe as being sugar-mindful, and in our ordinary, everyday lives, we consume less sugar than the average Swedish household according to current statistics.

Sugar is sugar, as some say, but personally, I am particularly wary of the sneaky hidden sugars of the cheap, processed kind most often found in packaged products, from ketchup to bread to whole grain cereal mixes. I don't presume to prescribe a certain way of eating to you, but I do subscribe to the obvious, simple truth that by making your own treats at home, you can decide what goes into them and what is omitted. The homemade treats you'll whip up using this book contain actual real food and plant-based ingredients, as opposed to some factory-made products with healthy sounding, greenwash-y names and illustrations on the packaging that reference nature, such as fruit and leaves. All the recipes here are 100 percent vegan, many have gluten-free options and many can be adapted to cater to allergy sufferers. What does this mean? Well, simply that more people can enjoy them. For a start, everyone can eat plant-based food! And, moreover, the making and sharing of treats and the taking of fika breaks is all about enjoyment. I truly believe that eating treats shouldn't be about having fun in the moment only to feel regretful or unwell minutes later.

If you compare the treats in this book to their more conventional counterparts, you will not only find them to be free of refined sugar, but you may notice with many that the sugar content in general is significantly lower. I don't obsess over numbers throughout this book because I don't in my personal life either, but for illustrative purposes, my kladdkaka, or gooey Swedish chocolate cake, contains 1 teaspoon of maple syrup plus ¼ teaspoon of banana-derived natural sugar per serving. In contrast, a single serving of traditional kladdkaka, with its common accompaniment of vanilla ice cream, can contain in excess of 14 teaspoons (59 g) of white sugar. Rather steep if you consider that the World Health Organization's (WHO) 2015 publication "Guideline: Sugars intake for adults and children" recommended adults and children reduce their daily intake of free sugars to less than 10 percent of their total energy intake, adding that a further reduction to below 5 percent per day would provide additional health benefits. Less than 5 percent sugar consumption per person, per day, amounts to around 6 teaspoons (25 g) of sugar!

Put simply, if you're eating a generally wholesome diet, you can have your naturally sweet version of kladdkaka, and eat it too, while still observing WHO's guidelines, if that is important to you.

Although I would dearly love for these treats to be appreciated not only by your taste buds, but your body too, this publication is not intended to serve as a diet book or a nutritional program. And though it is widely believed that reducing the amount of sugar and heavily processed foods in our diets is health affirming for everybody and every body, this is essentially a collection of recipes that provides alternatives for those who want or need them.

As a result of the multicultural nature of my family and my intercontinental experiences, the recipes here are diverse in terms of both nostalgic inspiration and cultural influence. I wanted these recipes to reflect how we really eat—balanced and incorporating whole foods—and be indicative of the things I truly love to make for my family. If my kids didn't like a recipe I tested while writing this book, it did not make the cut. You may have children or you may not, but regardless, you probably know that a child's summation of the food they're presented is no-holds-barred! That being said, even within my own little family, each child has their own particular likes, dislikes and preferences.

To make these recipes more accessible and practical, I have tried to base them around easy-to-source ingredients. In fact, all the ingredients used to test these recipes were purchased from my own modestly-stocked local supermarket. I have taken into consideration common kitchen tools and appliances too, so, where possible, you can use an oven instead of a dehydrator, or a food processor instead of a high-powered blender.

I hope this book will become a go-to resource for the creation of sweet treats on the more wholesome side of the spectrum and one that is enjoyably accessible to people of all levels of cooking; vegans and non-vegans, folks who are sugar mindful, and the plant-based or low-sugar curious alike.

Love,

—Marisa

Measurements

All of the recipes in this book are written to include standard US cup measurements plus metric gram measurements for dry ingredients and metric milliliter measurements for wet ingredients, which have been rounded up appropriately, as per common written recipe convention. I understand the convenience of measuring cups, but I do advocate weighing ingredients for better accuracy and consistency, especially when making bread-based recipes. Where inch measurements are mentioned, so are millimeters. Temperatures are written in degrees Fahrenheit and Celsius. In this way I hope to be able to keep things simple and not have you constantly referring to conversion charts.

Sweeteners

Over the past 6-plus years, I have experimented with all manner of table sugar substitutes, from rice malt syrup to xylitol to spoon-for-spoon sugar replacers. For the purpose of this book, however, I most often refer to sweeteners that are widely accessible and as close to their natural, unrefined state as possible.

Here you'll find recipes that feature nuts, coconut, spices, vegetables, fruit, maple syrup, coconut sugar and, in a few instances, stevia as sweeteners. I am under no illusion that coconut sugar (or any form of sugar) is a healthy food, but, interestingly, coconut sugar does contain the prebiotic inulin, and it contains less fructose. Importantly, for vegans wanting to avoid products filtered with animal bone char, coconut sugar is never processed with it. These reasons, combined with the fact that it doesn't add extra moisture to batter and dough, warranted its inclusion. As an added bonus, its natural caramel notes mean you can add less of the sweetener and yet maintain a richness of flavor in baked goods. For those of you who can't find coconut sugar, simply replace it with brown sugar to maintain the same approximate flavor profile, or with a spoon-for-spoon granulated natural sweetener of your choice. Note that non-organic brown and white sugars can be processed with bone char, so check your sources or buy organic if this is an issue for you. While many companies use bone char, others do not. And guidelines may differ from country to country, but certified United States Department of Agriculture organic sugars cannot legally be processed with bone char and are therefore deemed vegan.

Although it has been processed, I personally find that, in modest quantities, organic rice malt syrup (or brown rice syrup) can be an excellent alternative to Swedish ljus sirap, the light syrup commonly used in baked goods here, English golden syrup and honey. As it is virtually impossible to find rice malt syrup here, I decided against writing it into the main recipes, opting instead to use pure organic maple syrup. Fructose-conscious friends, you will come across rice malt syrup as a listed optional substitute in some recipes, but note that you can substitute maple syrup for organic rice malt syrup when you come across it. If you have a preferred natural syrup other than maple, experiment with it.

Chocolate makes an appearance in some of the recipes, as you may well expect, and my personal preference is to use dairy-free chocolate of the super dark 85 to 90 percent cocoa variety. You may use the chocolate of your choice, including the raw, refined-sugar-free varieties, but the simple rule of thumb with chocolate is this: the greater the cocoa content, the lower the amount of sugar.

To differentiate natural sweetness that comes directly from plants in the form of fruits, vegetables or spices from other forms of sweetener, I refer to liquid and powder form sweeteners like maple syrup, coconut sugar and stevia as added sweeteners. So when you come across a recipe that has no added sweetener, it means that sweetness is derived directly from a plant source such as banana, and no extra sweetener has been added to it in the form of stevia, maple syrup or coconut sugar.

Dairy Alternatives

Obviously none of these recipes contain butter, but I have deliberately chosen to use natural alternatives rather than margarine or synthetic imitation buttery spreads. In this book you will find butter replacements most often in the form of nuts, nut butter, coconut butter, coconut oil, olive oil and avocado, all of which can be found in raw, unrefined or organic varieties. As a family, we are not oil-free eaters, but we lean towards the use of so-called healthy fats in modest amounts. These recipes reflect that, containing reduced amounts of oil in general. If, however, you'd prefer to use coconut butter, which is made from coconut flesh and is technically a whole food, instead of coconut oil, simply substitute it in the equivalent amount required, making sure to stir it well before measuring and adding. The finished texture of baked goods may vary slightly, but it is an easy switch to make.

When it comes to milk, I most often suggest almond, cashew, oat or coconut milk, as all are commonly found or can be made at home if necessary. But really, with the exception of canned organic coconut milk, which is the best thing I have found to replace dairy cream, the milks are largely interchangeable with any type of plant milk you prefer.

Naturally Sweet Vegan Treats

Egg Replacers

Eggs, butter and other animal-derived ingredients add moisture and body to baked goods and improve their texture. Removing them means finding suitable plant-based substitutions, and those listed here are easy to source and are reliable options. You will come across several ingredients that act as egg replacers in this book.

For binding, I most often use:

- Cornstarch
- Arrowroot powder or tapioca flour
- Agar-agar
- Nut butters
- Aquafaba (unsalted canned chickpea liquid)
- Chia seeds or flaxseeds

Aquafaba is the unsalted liquid from canned chickpeas. Ideally, aquafaba as an egg replacer should be the same consistency of egg whites in order for it to function effectively. If it is too watery, reduce it by a quarter by simmering it gently in a pan over low heat. Allow it to cool before incorporating it in your recipe.

The use of chia seeds as an egg substitute varies per recipe. Please note that each individual recipe's requirements don't always match the standard equation of one part chia seeds to three parts water. In this book the seeds are measured before grinding.

I tend to favor ground chia seeds over flaxseeds as I prefer the taste, finding it to be more neutral. Though, by all means, use flaxseeds if you prefer them. I prepare ground chia and flax seeds by blitzing the seeds to a powder in a small food processor or, most often, in an electric coffee bean grinder with blades. It takes seconds.

For adding moisture, I use:
- Cooked pumpkin purée
- Unsweetened applesauce
- Mashed ripe banana
- Cooked sweet potato purée
- Plant-based yogurts, most often coconut or oat
- Organic silken tofu

For leavening, I use combinations of:
- Baking powder
- Baking soda
- Apple cider vinegar
- Lemon juice

A Sweet Start

Pancakes, porridges, waffles and more

Roasted Peach & Banana Pancakes

Gluten-free with nut-free option | Makes 10-14 small pancakes

Roasted peaches have always held a romantic fascination for me on account of a favorite childhood storybook, *The Maggie B*. A girl named Margaret Barnstable wishes for a ship named after her. In the morning, she awakens aboard the *Maggie B*. and sets sail. That evening she whips up a batch of muffins, and pops some peaches into the oven. Of all the things that left an impression on me from this beloved tale, it was little Margaret's intuitive flair with ingredients—in particular the peaches—that captivated me. Roasting peaches enhances both their wonderful flavor and natural sweetness, making them a perfect pancake partner. Prep the peaches and pop them in the oven to roast while you whip up the pancakes. You'll feel as capable as Margaret Barnstable!

This recipe is dedicated to my dad: He introduced me to the magic of both books and banana pancakes.

Roasted Peaches

3 cups (600 g) peeled, sliced peaches, fresh or canned in juice

1 tsp coconut sugar, optional

½ tsp ground cinnamon

¼ tsp pure vanilla powder

Pinch of ground nutmeg

Peach & Banana Pancakes

1½ cups + 2 tbsp (385 ml) unsweetened cashew milk

¼ cup + 1 tbsp (75 ml) mashed ripe banana

¼ cup + 1 tbsp (75 ml) puréed peaches

2 tbsp (30 ml) coconut oil, melted

1 tbsp (15 ml) maple syrup

1 tsp vanilla extract

1 tsp apple cider vinegar

2 cups (240 g) buckwheat flour, spelt or all-purpose organic flour

1 tbsp (14 g) baking powder

½ tsp ground cinnamon

Olive or coconut oil for frying (or use a non-stick pan)

¼ cup (30 g) chopped pecans or flaked almonds, for serving, optional

To roast the peaches, preheat the oven to 350°F (180°C). If using canned peaches, drain the juice and reserve it to add to smoothies or oatmeal. Arrange the peach slices in a large parchment paper–lined baking dish in a single layer. Mix the sugar (if using), cinnamon, vanilla and nutmeg together and sprinkle over the peach slices. Bake the peaches for 20 to 30 minutes or until cooked through and caramelized to your liking.

While the peaches roast, prepare the pancakes by adding the milk, banana, peaches, oil, syrup, vanilla and vinegar to a large mixing bowl, stirring to combine. Add the buckwheat flour, baking powder and cinnamon to the wet mix and stir to incorporate.

Heat the oil in a frying pan over medium heat.

Ladle the batter into the pan—to make small pancakes, a ladle containing 3 tablespoons (45 ml) of batter works well. Cook each pancake for 3 minutes or until you see the edges have cooked and small bubbles are forming on the surface. Flip and cook each pancake on the other side for 2 to 3 minutes until done. Repeat until all the batter is used.

Serve the pancakes hot, topped with the roasted peach slices and nuts or other toppings of choice.

Recipe Note: To make the pancakes nut-free, use coconut milk in place of cashew milk and use toasted coconut in place of nuts to serve.

Chocolate Cake Batter Waffles

Gluten-free option | Makes 4 waffles and ¹/₂ cup (120 ml) fudge sauce

Taking the waffle game to the next level, here we have chocolate cake batter waffles speckled with crunchy cacao, and served up with Chocolate Fudge Sauce. This waffle recipe produces a thick batter that works well in both waffle irons and silicone molds. If using a waffle iron, my preferred method for cooking these waffles, you can expect a pleasantly crisp waffle with a satisfyingly toothsome texture. If you'd rather use molds to make them, the finished texture will be enjoyable waffle-meets-muffin-like. Charles M. Schulz famously said, "All you need is love. But a little chocolate now and then doesn't hurt." I am inclined to agree.

Chocolate Fudge Sauce

¼ cup (25 g) raw cacao powder

2–3 tbsp (30–45 ml) maple syrup, to taste

2–3 tbsp (30–45 ml) coconut oil

½ tsp pure vanilla powder

Chocolate Waffles

1¼ cups (160 g) spelt flour

¼ cup (25 g) pure unsweetened cocoa powder

¼ cup (35 g) coconut sugar

1½ tsp (7 g) baking powder

1 tbsp (9 g) cornstarch

⅛ tsp salt

⅓ cup (80 ml) light olive oil or other neutral oil

⅓ cup + 3 tbsp (125 ml) oat or nut milk

⅓ cup (80 ml) aquafaba, whisked until foamy and slightly thickened

1 tbsp (15 ml) water

1 tsp vanilla extract

1 tbsp (15 ml) apple cider vinegar

3 tbsp (27 g) cacao nibs, optional

Coconut Whip (page 183), nice-cream and fresh berries, to serve, optional

To make the chocolate fudge sauce, mix the cacao, syrup, oil and vanilla in a small saucepan over low heat and stir until the coconut oil has melted and everything is well combined. If the sauce is too thick for your liking, add a little extra coconut oil and stir until the desired consistency is achieved. Best served warm, this sauce can be reheated gently if the mix starts to solidify slightly. Set the sauce to the side.

Preheat the waffle iron.

Whisk together the flour, cocoa, sugar, baking powder, cornstarch and salt. Add the oil, milk, aquafaba, water, vanilla and vinegar to the dry ingredients. Fold together until the ingredients are combined. Allow the batter to sit for 5 minutes so the baking powder can activate properly—it will begin to look like chocolate mousse. Gently fold in the cacao nibs if using.

If using a waffle iron, grease it with coconut oil if required. Spoon the batter into the waffle iron and cook the waffles according to manufacturer specifications.

To make these waffles in silicone molds, preheat the oven to 430°F (220°C). Grease the molds with melted coconut oil or butter. Place the molds on a baking tray and fill each a little over three-quarters full. Bake for 8 minutes on the center rack of the oven. Allow the waffles to cool in the molds for 10 minutes before turning them onto a parchment paper-lined tray. Place the tray in the oven for 2 to 3 minutes to allow the upturned waffles to crisp up.

Serve the freshly made waffles with Coconut Whip, non-dairy ice cream, a drizzle of Chocolate Fudge Sauce and fruit or berries, if you like.

Recipe Note: To make the waffles gluten-free, use gluten-free all-purpose flour in place of spelt.

Naturally Sweet Vegan Treats

Pumpkin Spice Pumpkin Pancakes

Fructose-, nut-, gluten- and oil-free options |
Makes 10-12 small pancakes

Big on comfort and super low on sugar, these delicious spice-laced, plant-based pancakes are easy to prepare and great with all manner of toppings. If, like me, you find the changing of seasons and the darkening of days a somewhat melancholy proposition, cheer yourself and treat your tummy to a truly festive autumnal breakfast. You can adjust the amount of spice to your liking, but I personally find the balance here makes these pancakes versatile when it comes to toppings and palatable for both adults and children.

1¾ cups (225 g) organic all-purpose flour or gluten-free flour blend

1½ tbsp (21 g) baking powder

Pinch of salt

1½ tsp (4 g) ground cinnamon

¼ tsp ground nutmeg

¼ tsp ground ginger

Pinch of ground cloves

½ cup (120 g) pure pumpkin purée

1 tbsp (15 ml) coconut oil, melted + extra for the pan

1 tbsp (15 ml) maple syrup or rice malt syrup, optional

1 tsp vanilla extract

1¾ cups (420 ml) nut or oat milk + extra if needed

Coconut Whip (page 183), pecans, Raw Toffee Spread (page 191), to serve, optional

Combine the flour, baking powder, salt, cinnamon, nutmeg, ginger and cloves in a large bowl, giving them a whisk with a fork or wire whisk.

Combine the pumpkin, oil, syrup (if using), vanilla and milk in a medium-size mixing bowl, and then add the wet mix to the dry ingredients.

Fold through just until blended, but try not to overmix. If the batter seems too thick at this point, add a little extra milk to the mix and fold it in.

Heat a lightly oiled large skillet/frying pan over medium-high heat.

Using a ⅓-cup (80-ml) measure or a small ladle, scoop the batter in even amounts into the pan and cook each pancake for 3 minutes or until bubbles start to form on the surface and the edges appear dry. You should be able to cook 2 pancakes at a time using this method and measure. Flip the pancakes over and cook for 2 to 3 minutes or until they are brown on the other side. Repeat this process until all the batter is used.

Serve these pancakes warm with a drizzle of syrup and some Coconut Whip, pecans and Raw Toffee Spread, or other combinations of toppings of choice.

Recipe Notes: To make the pancakes oil-free, replace the coconut oil with an extra tablespoon (15 g) of pumpkin purée or coconut butter and cook the pancakes in a nonstick skillet.

To make the pancakes with no added natural sweetener, omit the syrup.

Simple Baked Waffles

No added natural sweetener, nut- and gluten-free options |
Makes 4 full-sized waffles or 20 minis

Delicately crisp on the outside, fluffy in the middle and extra easy to whip up using silicone waffle molds, the flavor of these waffles is as close to the classic Swedish-style iron-cooked waffle as I have made—minus the waffle iron, dairy, sugar or eggs! The addition of spelt to the batter adds to the crispiness of these waffles, while the neutral flavor profile allows you to dress them up in any manner you fancy. By using silicone molds to make them, you can bake the entire batch of waffles in one go and face an easy clean-up operation afterwards. Luxurious and lazy Sunday breakfast, anyone?

Melted coconut oil for greasing

1¼ cups (155 g) organic all-purpose flour

¾ cup (85 g) oat flour, packed and levelled

1½ cups (60 g) spelt flour

1½ tsp baking soda

Pinch of salt

1 cup (240 ml) oat, almond or cashew milk

⅔ cup (160 ml) cold water

¼ cup (60 ml) unsweetened apple sauce

4 tsp (20 ml) melted coconut oil or olive oil

1 tsp vanilla extract

⅓ cup aquafaba, whisked until soft, fluffy and lightly peaked

Coconut Whip (page 183), Jams (pages 188–191), chocolate spreads (pages 195–197) or fresh fruit or berries, to serve, optional

Preheat the oven to 430°F (220°C). Make sure the silicone molds are very clean. Brush them lightly with melted coconut oil and place them on a baking tray. Line another baking tray with parchment paper.

Combine the 3 flours, baking soda and salt in a large mixing bowl. In a medium-size mixing bowl, combine the milk, water, apple sauce, oil and vanilla. Use a wire whisk to mix until the batter is smooth and lump-free. Spoon in the aquafaba and whisk it through the batter until incorporated. Spoon the waffle batter into the prepared molds.

Bake the waffles for 8 minutes or until golden. Remove the baking tray with waffle molds from the oven, keeping in mind that the silicone will be very hot to touch at first. Allow the waffles to cool in the molds for 10 minutes. Carefully unmold the waffles, using oven gloves if necessary. Flip them over onto the parchment-lined baking tray, and pop them back in the oven for 2 to 5 minutes to allow the other side to toast. Keep an eye on the waffles to prevent overbaking.

Remove the waffles from the oven when done to your liking and serve them immediately with your toppings of choice.

Recipe Notes: Larger grid silicone molds may produce waffles that need more than 5 minutes in the second bake to crisp up and cook through.

These waffles can also be made using a waffle iron. Cook them per your iron's specifications.

Naturally Sweet Vegan Treats

Coconut-Crusted French Toast

Nut-free with gluten-free and no added sweetener options | Makes 6 slices or 3-6 servings

Served with caramelized pineapple, this luscious morning indulgence was inspired by a breakfast date long ago in Adelaide with one of my biggest influences: artist, author, restaurateur and runner-up of MasterChef Australia's first season Poh Ling Yeow. On my plate that day was the most amazing coconut-crusted French toast. Goodness only knows why the café we dined in later removed their version from the menu, but I recreated the basic flavors with my own vegan version, and won a competition hosted by television cook Alice Zaslavsky in the process. The recipe itself was never shared publicly in its entirety—until now.

Want to know a simple way to increase the natural sweetness in fruit without adding extra sugar? Caramelize it! Not only is this caramelized pineapple delicious in conjunction with this tropical take on French toast, it's great with oatmeal, on chia puddings and even added to salads!

Coconut oil for frying, divided

6 slices fresh or canned-in-juice organic pineapple

1 tbsp (14 g) chia seeds, finely ground + 3 tbsp (45 ml) water

2 tsp (6 g) arrowroot powder or cornstarch

1⅓ cups (325 ml) full-fat organic coconut milk

1 tbsp (15 ml) maple syrup + extra for serving, optional

1 tsp vanilla extract

Pinch of salt

1¼ cups (155 g) unsweetened desiccated coconut

6 slices of sourdough or other sturdy bread, sliced just shy of an inch (20 mm)

Coconut yogurt and finely grated lime zest for serving

Preheat the oven to 250°F (120°C). In a large nonstick skillet/frying pan over medium to medium-high heat, add 1 tablespoon (15 ml) of coconut oil. Place the pineapple rings in the pan, and cook them for 3 to 4 minutes per side until browned and caramelized. Place the slices in an oven-safe dish and pop them in the oven to keep warm.

Rinse out and dry the frying pan so it's ready to reuse. Mix the chia seeds and water in a small glass bowl. Mix well and briskly with a teaspoon. The mix should start to jell almost immediately.

Add the chia mix, arrowroot, milk, syrup (if using), vanilla and salt to a food processor/blender and give everything a whizz to combine well. This can also be done by placing the ingredients in a large bowl and whisking to incorporate them.

Tip the batter into a shallow dish wide enough to fit a slice of bread. Spread the desiccated coconut onto a large plate.

Dip both sides of each slice of bread into the batter to just coat it, but do not soak it or the bread will be soggy.

Place both sides of the batter-coated bread into the desiccated coconut to coat them.

Place the nonstick frying pan back onto the stove over medium heat, adding 1 tablespoon (15 ml) of coconut oil and two slices of the coated bread.

(continued)

Coconut-Crusted French Toast (Continued)

Drizzle a small amount of batter over the coated bread slices as they fry to help the coconut adhere to the top of the bread before you flip it over. Cook each slice for 4 to 5 minutes until it turns a toasty golden brown color, and use a spatula to flip it over and cook for another 4 to 5 minutes.

When the first slices are done, keep them warm by placing them in an ovenproof dish on the center rack of the oven next to the cooked pineapple slices. Repeat the French toast cooking process, adding a tablespoon (15 ml) of coconut oil to the pan for each 2 new slices of bread, until all the toast is made.

Serve the slices immediately topped with the warm pineapple, some coconut yogurt and grated lime zest. Add a little drizzle of maple syrup, if you like.

Recipe Note: Gluten-free sourdough bread, or a sturdier gluten-free bread of choice, may be used.

Pull-Apart Chocolate Chip Oatmeal Bread

Warning: This bread is so yummy that it is hard to stop at one piece. However, with just 2 tablespoons (30 ml) of sweetener in the entire tray of 24 rolls, you can definitely enjoy another slice. This is my family's answer to the triangular pull-apart oat bread that can be found on supermarket shelves in stores across Sweden. The store-bought variety contains three types of sugar in the form of white sugar, syrup and added fruit sugar even though oat bread is not considered a sweet bread. And, to be very honest, I really do prefer our moist, fluffy and far-less-sweet version. The chocolate chips are entirely optional, of course, and this bread is wonderful without them, too. Currants and walnuts make wonderful alternative add-ins. Left plain, this bread is perfect for savory sandwiches or to serve toasty and warm with a bowl of soup. Whip up a tray and delight friends and family with this wonderful addition to any breakfast, lunch or afternoon tea spread!

---

2 cups (250 g) spelt flour, packed and leveled

2 cups (320 g) organic all-purpose flour, packed and leveled + an extra ½ cup (80 g) as needed

1¾ tbsp (14 g) instant yeast

1¾ cups (160 g) rolled oats

3¼ cups (780 ml) oat milk, divided

1 tsp of salt

¼ cup + 1 tbsp (75 ml) light olive oil

1 tsp maple syrup

½ cup (75 g) dairy-free chopped dark chocolate or chocolate chips, optional

Line a deep-sided oven tray with a sheet of parchment paper. Whatever tray best fits your oven will work, but 12 × 16 inches (30 × 40 cm) should be ideal.

Add the spelt and all-purpose flour to a large mixing bowl, then stir in the instant yeast. Allow the flour and yeast mix to sit for 10 minutes without liquid, as I find this aids the activation process.

In a medium-size saucepan, combine the oats with 2 cups (480 ml) of oat milk and the salt. Cook over low-medium heat, stirring occasionally, for 3 minutes or until thickened slightly. Remove the pan from the heat.

Stir the olive oil and maple syrup into the cooked oats, then add the remaining 1¼ cups (300 ml) of oat milk and allow the mixture to come to finger-warm temperature. This is important because if it is too warm or too cold, the yeast may not activate the way it should, thus affecting the rise of the bread.

(continued)

Pull-Apart Chocolate Chip Oatmeal Bread (Continued)

Pop the oat mix into a bowl of a stand mixer with a dough hook attachment. You can attempt this process by hand, but it will take considerably more effort, of course. Start the mixer on a low-medium speed and begin to add the flour and yeast mixture, a spoon at a time until it is all incorporated. The mix should become smooth and elastic. Allow it to knead for 5 minutes. Note that because of the oatmeal the dough will remain rather sticky, but it should come together. If the dough doesn't come away from the sides of the mixing bowl easily when you scrape them down with a silicone spatula, continue to add up to an extra ½ cup (80 g) of all-purpose flour, a little at a time. Mix in the chocolate, if using.

Let the dough rise in the bowl, covered with a clean tea towel, for 30 minutes.

Tip the dough onto the lined tray and use your hands and the aid of a silicone spatula to flatten the dough out evenly to form a rectangle about 11¼ × 15 inches (28 × 38 cm). The neater and more even your dough rectangle is, the more uniform each bread triangle will be, but a little rustic charm never hurt anyone.

Using a pizza slicer, knife or dough scraper, slice the dough into 12 squares of 3¾ inches (95 mm). Then slice through each square on the diagonal to produce 24 triangles. Allow the dough to rise again, covered by a clean tea towel, for another 30 minutes. Towards the end of the proofing time, preheat the oven to 425°F (220°C).

Bake the bread for 18 to 20 minutes or until it is baked through and the top turns a golden brown color. Allow the bread to cool for at least 15 minutes.

Recipe Notes: In the case of yeasted bread recipes in particular, I always advocate weighing over measuring with cups if possible, as even small deviations of amounts can adversely affect the finished product.

If you don't have spelt flour, you can replace it by using 4 cups (640 g) of organic all-purpose flour, packed and leveled, plus up to an extra ½ cup (80 g) if required.

This bread can be frozen for up to 3 months.

Naturally Sweet Vegan Treats

Quick "Buttermilk" Flatbreads

No added unrefined sweetener, nut- and oil-free options | Makes 8 individual flatbreads

Think tasty flatbread meets English muffin, and you're basically imagining these rustic breakfast treats—the perfect vehicle for your favorite toast toppers! Commercially prepared bread, including the whole-grain supermarket varieties, can contain up to three different types of added sugar without even appearing noticeably sweet. So if you like bread for breakfast, and particularly like the idea of one that skimps on the added sweetener, this easy-to-make recipe is your new friend; just minutes to prep, no rising time needed and 10 to 14 minutes for cooking. These flatbreads are dedicated to my friends who are time-poor and nervy about using yeast! You'll be hard-pressed to find a quicker, easier bread recipe with no added sweetener that tastes so delicious.

⅓ cup + 1 tbsp (95 ml) coconut or oat yogurt

⅓ cup + 1 tbsp (95 ml) nut or oat milk

1 tsp apple cider vinegar

¼ cup (60 ml) coconut oil or coconut butter, melted

2 cups (260 g) organic all-purpose flour

1½ tsp (7 g) baking powder

¼ to ½ tsp salt, according to taste

Basic Strawberry Chia Jam (page 191) or Chocolate & Peanut Butter Fudge Topping (page 195), to serve, optional

In a medium-size mixing bowl, combine the yogurt, milk and vinegar. In a large mixing bowl, combine the oil, flour, baking powder and salt. Pour the flour mixture over the milk mixture and bring the ingredients together to form a dough.

Divide the dough into 8 pieces and use your hands to roll each piece into a rough ball. Flatten each ball into rounds approximately ⅓ inch (8 mm) thick.

Heat a skillet or a frying pan over medium heat. Do not add any oil to the pan. Instead, sprinkle a small amount of flour into the pan before placing the flatbreads into it. A larger pan should be able to fit 4 pieces at a time. Cook them for 3 to 4 minutes, flipping them over when golden brown patches have appeared. Cook for 2 to 3 minutes further on the other side, adjusting the heat if necessary to prevent burning.

These breads are delicious served with Basic Strawberry Chia Jam or Chocolate & Peanut Butter Fudge Topping.

Recipe Notes: The organic all-purpose flour can be replaced with 2 cups (245 g) of spelt flour, for those who prefer it, or a half-and-half mix of 1 cup spelt flour (122 g) and 1 cup (130 g) all-purpose flour.

Leftover breads can be stored, once cooled, in an airtight container in the freezer for up to 3 months.

Coconut Butter Brioche

Nut-free option | Makes 9 buns

When I was a little girl, my parents very graciously allowed me to bake in our kitchen without recipes or instruction. In fact, my very first attempts at recipe-less baking took place at around age six, and, as you can imagine, there were a few failures. On one occasion, though, something magical and unexpected happened. What could have been an unmitigated disaster of thrown together random quantities of ingredients resulted in something that earned the hearty praise of my parents. It wasn't the cake I had anticipated, but as my parents tasted and appraised my creation, I heard the exotic word "brioche" for the first time. I didn't know what brioche was, but I knew that it was good.

Many years later, in pastry school, I was taught a delightful egg- and butter-filled traditional version. And now, in a full circle kind of way, I have taken experimental liberties yet again—the result being a rich yet light vegan version of a bread that makes the perfect breakfast companion. My vegan husband adores these buns just as they are. I enjoy them served with nut butters and dairy-free spreads.

¼ cup (50 g) coconut butter, well stirred and at room temperature

3 tbsp + 1 tsp (50 ml) olive oil

½ cup (120 ml) oat or nut milk

1–3 tbsp (15–45 ml) oat, coconut or soy yogurt, divided

1½ tbsp (14 g) coconut sugar

0.7 oz (20 g) fresh, refrigerated yeast for sweet dough

2 cups (320 g) organic all-purpose flour, completely packed and leveled

¼ tsp salt

Glaze
1 tbsp (9 g) coconut sugar

2 tsp (10 ml) freshly boiled water

In a small saucepan, gently melt the coconut butter. Add the oil, milk, 1 tablespoon (15 ml) yogurt and sugar, then let the mix cool to a finger-warm temperature. Stir in the yeast until it dissolves.

Add the carefully measured flour and salt to the bowl of a stand mixer or a large mixing bowl.

Pour in the milk mixture and begin combining the ingredients with a dough hook on low speed. Once the flour is mostly incorporated, check to see if the mix is moist enough. The mix should come together to produce a smooth, elastic and moist dough. Add a tablespoon (15 ml) of yogurt if needed. Adjust the speed on your stand mixer to medium and allow the dough to be kneaded for 5 minutes. If doing this process without a stand mixer, knead the dough by hand for 10 minutes.

Form the dough into a rough ball and place it back in the bowl. Cover the bowl with a tea towel and allow the dough to rise for 1 to 1½ hours or until doubled in size. Line a 9-inch (23-cm) springform pan for round rolls or square pan for square rolls with parchment paper.

After the dough has doubled, punch it down, then shape it into a log and divide it into 9 pieces of equal weight. Shape each dough piece into a ball and place them into the lined pan. Cover the pan with a clean tea towel and allow the buns to proof for 40 minutes, around the end of which time you can preheat the oven to 340°F (170°C) convection or 350°F (180°C) non-convection.

(continued)

Naturally Sweet Vegan Treats

Coconut Butter Brioche (Continued)

Bake the buns for about 18 minutes or until golden brown on the surface and baked through.

While the buns are baking, prepare a glaze by combining the coconut sugar and freshly boiled water in a small bowl.

Remove the baked buns from the oven and brush with the glaze. Release the springform mechanism on the baking pan and transfer the buns carefully to a wire rack. Allow the buns to cool slightly before serving.

Recipe Notes: In the case of yeasted bread recipes in particular, I always advocate weighing over measuring with cups if possible, as even small deviations of amounts can adversely affect the finished product.

These buns are also lovely eaten cold and can be stored in an airtight container for up to 3 days, or frozen for later use for up to 3 months.

Naturally Sweet Vegan Treats

Pear & Blackberry Breakfast Pastries

Low added sweetener | Makes 4 to 5 pastries

A semi-sweet hand pie with cream "cheese" frosting for breakfast? Go on, treat yourself! When I first traveled to America as a nine-year-old, certain things that are now commonplace in Australia were an exotic culinary proposition. Brownies, Cap'n Crunch and Lucky Charms novelty cereals and Pop-Tarts all left lasting impressions. These days, I make my own versions of many of the treats I enjoyed during that trip. This is one such recipe. It's safe to say these homemade tarts are not of the toaster-friendly kind, so don't be tempted. They are, however, vegan, while commercially made Pop-Tarts are not in most cases, and these provide a naturally sweet, light and decidedly less sugary alternative to the novel and infamous breakfast pastry that inspired them. In a crunch for time? Use store-bought vegan pastry.

---

1 quantity Olive Oil Short Crust Pastry (page 175)

½ cup (120 ml) of Pear & Blackberry Jam with Agar-Agar (page 188)

1 tsp ground cinnamon for sprinkling, optional

2 tbsp (30 ml) creamy coconut milk

1 tbsp (9 g) coconut sugar

Cream "Cheese" Frosting

¾ cup (115 g) raw cashews, soaked 4 hours to overnight

2 tbsp (30 ml) water

1 tbsp (15 ml) melted coconut oil

4 tsp (20 ml) maple syrup

1 tsp vanilla extract

1 tsp lemon juice

Pinch of salt

¼ tsp ground cinnamon, optional

1–2 tsp berry or pitaya powder or beet juice for coloring, optional

Once the pastry dough has been made, wrap it in cling film or parchment paper and place it in the fridge to rest for 30 minutes.

After 30 minutes, unwrap the dough and pop it onto a sheet of parchment paper on a clean work surface. If it is not easily workable, allow it to come closer to room temperature. Place a second sheet of parchment paper on top of it and roll the dough into a rectangle about 1/16 inch (2 mm) thick. From this, cut 12 equal-size pastry rectangles of 3 x 4⅓ inches (75 × 110 mm) each.

Evenly space 6 of the pastry pieces on a parchment paper–lined baking tray.

Place 1 heaping tablespoon (20 ml) of jam in the center of each pastry piece and spread the jam out evenly, leaving a ½ inch (12 mm) border of dough all around the edges. If using cinnamon, sprinkle it lightly over the jam on the pastries. Brush a little water around the edge of each jam-topped pastry piece.

Gently place each of the 6 remaining pastry rectangles over the top of the jam and seal the edges by pressing them down firmly with your fingertips.

Use a fork to crimp all the edges (do this firmly but without dragging on the pastry) and to pierce the tops of each pastry 4 times. If the outer edges of the crimped pastry fringe look a little ragged, trim them slightly and carefully with a sharp knife to neaten them up.

Pear & Blackberry Breakfast Pastries (Continued)

(continued)

Place the unbaked pastries in the freezer for 1 hour. Preheat the oven to 350°F (180°C).

Remove the pastries from the freezer and brush them lightly with the creamy coconut milk. Sprinkle with the coconut sugar. Bake for 20 to 24 minutes or until golden brown and cooked through.

Prepare the frosting by draining the soaked cashews and popping them into a small food processor along with the water, oil, syrup, vanilla, lemon juice, salt and cinnamon (if using). Color the frosting by adding a teaspoon or two of berry powder, if you like. Blend until smooth.

Allow the tarts to cool completely before frosting. Pipe or spread the frosting onto the cooled tarts. Serve them immediately once they are frosted.

Recipe Notes: This recipe can be made super fast with store-bought vegan puff pastry. Follow the directions for cutting and assembling above, skipping the freezer time and omitting the coconut cream and sugar step.

Have fun with this recipe and experiment with alternative fillings such as Sautéed Apple Pie Filling (page 98), Basic Strawberry Chia Jam (page 191) or Tropical Curd (page 198).

In place of the Cream "Cheese" Frosting, you can also try Subtly Sweet Caramel Sauce (page 192), Chocolate & Peanut Butter Fudge Topping (page 195) or From-Scratch Basic Chocolate Ganache (page 196).

Spelt & Banana Breakfast Muffins

Oil-free option | Makes 5-6 muffins

Store-bought muffins have found themselves deemed amongst the most notorious of the seemingly-healthy-yet-actually-unhealthy breakfast options. Often laden with sneaky processed sugars, trans fats and empty calories, they're probably not the ideal option for sustainably boosting morning mood and energy levels. While spelt has some surprising health benefits, its taste and texture warranted its inclusion in this recipe. Low in oil and naturally sweetened, these humble breakfast muffins are lovely as they are and can be dressed up with a dollop of Pear & Blackberry Jam with Agar-Agar (page 188), Basic Strawberry Chia Jam (page 191) or the addition of fresh berries. This is a small-batch baking project, but double the quantities of ingredients to double the amount of muffins if you wish, and you'll have more light-yet-satisfying grab-and-go breakfast treats on hand!

1½ cups (175 g) spelt flour

¼ cup + 1 tbsp (45 g) coconut sugar

1½ tsp (7 g) baking powder

½ tsp baking soda

Pinch of salt

1 tsp ground cinnamon

½ cup (120 ml) oat, almond or cashew milk

½ cup (120 ml) mashed ripe banana, packed

3 tbsp (45 ml) coconut oil or coconut butter, melted

1 tsp vanilla extract

½ tsp apple cider vinegar

¼ cup (30 g) chopped walnuts

Preheat the oven to 350°F (180°C). Line a muffin pan with cupcake liners or lightly grease silicone muffin cups with a little coconut oil.

In a large mixing bowl, combine the flour, sugar, baking powder and soda, salt and cinnamon. In a small mixing bowl combine the milk, banana, oil, vanilla and vinegar and add it to the dry ingredients. Fold the wet mix through the dry to combine until no flour shows, but do not overmix.

Spoon the batter into the cupcake liners, filling each to three-quarters capacity. Top each muffin with a sprinkle of chopped walnuts.

Bake the muffins for about 20 to 25 minutes or until a toothpick inserted in the center of a muffin comes out clean.

Carefully transfer the baked muffins to a wire rack and allow them to cool at least slightly before serving. They're delicious warm or cold.

Buckwheat & Apricot Granola

Gluten- and grain-free with oil-free option | Makes about 4 cups (700 g)

There is little more comforting or welcoming to me breakfast-wise than homemade granola fresh from the oven. A wholesome and addictively delicious interpretation, this recipe is dedicated to my friend Ashley, quite possibly the best granola maker in the Australian state of Victoria. I was encouraged to start making my own granola again after a much-needed rejuvenating stay in Ashley's beautiful country home, where I also had the chance to reflect on the fact that there's a lot to be said for the restorative powers of kindness, a good breakfast and a little self-nurture. I hope this flavorful, chewy-meets-crunchy granola inspired by Ashley's makes you and yours feel warm, fuzzy and cared for, too.

---

1 cup (90 g) desiccated coconut

½ cup (65 g) pecans

½ cup (65 g) walnuts

¾ cup (145 g) soft organic dried apricots, chopped

⅓ cup (60 g) pitted medjool dates, chopped

2 tbsp (30 ml) cashew or almond butter

2 tbsp (30 ml) coconut oil or coconut butter

2 tbsp (35 ml) maple syrup

3 tbsp (45 g) mashed ripe banana

1 tsp pure vanilla powder

Pinch of salt

½ cup (65 g) chopped almonds

1 cup (170 g) activated buckwheat groats

Preheat the oven to 350°F (180°C) and line a large baking tray with parchment paper.

In a food processor, pulse the coconut, pecans, walnuts, apricots and dates until they form a rough and tacky dough.

In a small pan over low heat, gently melt together the butter, oil and syrup. Add in the banana, vanilla and salt, stirring to combine. Allow the mix to cool slightly.

Add the pulsed fruit, almonds and buckwheat groats to a large mixing bowl. Then pour the butter mix into the bowl and stir to combine well. Spread the mixture evenly and thinly over the parchment-lined tray.

Bake the mix for about 20 minutes, breaking it up a bit with a spoon and turning the tray around halfway through the bake time. Once golden brown and fragrant, remove the granola from the oven and allow it to cool completely.

Serve the granola in modest amounts—a little goes a long way—with coconut yogurt or a plant milk of your choice. Top with fresh berries, if you like.

Recipe Notes: For an oil-free option, replace the coconut oil with an equivalent amount of coconut butter.

Store leftover granola in the fridge for up to a week or in the freezer for up to 3 months.

Golden Milk Hot Chocolate Oats

Low-fructose with nut-, oil- and gluten-free options | Makes 2 generous servings

Warm cocoa meets fortifying spices and oatmeal in a simple, sustaining, comforting breakfast bowl with benefits. Some describe hot cocoa as "a hug in a mug." But add comforting oatmeal and the warming spices of anti-inflammatory turmeric-infused golden milk to the mix, and a wholesome, next level cozy-yet-energy-boosting breakfast awaits! I have also found this chocolaty, barely sweetened breakfast makes a great wet weather mood-improver.

Golden Milk Hot Chocolate

1 cup (240 ml) unsweetened nut or coconut milk, or a combination of both

2 tbsp (15 g) raw cacao powder or pure unsweetened cocoa powder

1 tsp ground turmeric

½ tsp ground ginger

Pinch of pure vanilla powder

1 tsp maple syrup (or to taste)

A crack of freshly ground black pepper

1 tsp organic coconut oil, optional

Oatmeal

1 cup (100 g) rolled oats

1 cup (240 ml) unsweetened oat, nut or coconut milk

1 cup (240 ml) water + extra if needed

Tiny pinch of salt, optional

In one small- to medium-size saucepan, warm the milk gently over low heat. Sift in the cacao, turmeric, ginger and vanilla, whisking well to combine. Add the maple syrup and whisk it through to incorporate. Add a crack of black pepper.

Taste to see if any adjustment needs to be made. My taste buds have acclimated over time to low-sweetener foods of all kinds, but if this way of eating is new to you, add a touch more maple syrup if you feel it's needed. In time, if you eat in a reduced-sugar manner, you will find that you can cut back even more on all kinds of sweeteners.

Once the milk is heated thoroughly and the ingredients are well combined, add the coconut oil, if using, and stir. Turn the stove heat down to the lowest setting and leave until the mix is required.

In a separate saucepan add the oats, pour in the milk and water and sprinkle in the salt (if using). Bring the oatmeal to a boil, and then reduce the heat and simmer for about 4 minutes or until it reaches the desired consistency, stirring from time to time to ensure it doesn't stick to the bottom of the pan.

Divide the oatmeal between two bowls and pour half the hot chocolate mix over one portion and the rest over the other. Stir a little to combine.

Recipe Notes: For a fructose-free option, use 1 teaspoon of rice malt syrup in place of maple syrup.

To make this nut-free, use oat or coconut milk.

To make this breakfast gluten-free, use coconut or nut milk and gluten-free oats.

Naturally Sweet Vegan Treats

Sweet Potato Pie Baked Porridge for Two

Oil- and gluten-free with no added unrefined sweetener and nut-free options | Serves 2

Let it be known, I am rather obsessed with porridge. And I have a major thing for sweet potatoes and the fragrant spices found in every self-respecting Swedish pantry. So this recipe is everything I could want in a nourishing breakfast! Think along the lines of sweet potato pie in the form of a bowl of oatmeal meets a spiced muffin fresh from the oven. It might sound strange, but trust me on this one. This baked porridge is gluten-free, oil-free and even fruit-free (for those minding their fructose intake) and can be made completely unrefined sweetener-free too. The most important thing to me and my kids, however, is that these baked breakfast treats are yummy, satisfying and warmingly comforting. There's plenty here for little ones to get involved with prep-wise too, from the measuring of dry ingredients to the mashing of sweet potato. Actually, I am not sure what my kids like more, the process of making it or the end result.

2 tsp (10 ml) melted coconut oil for greasing, optional

1 cup (95 g) gluten-free rolled oats

1 tsp baking powder

1½ tsp (4 g) ground cinnamon

¼ tsp ground nutmeg

¼ tsp ground cardamom

¼ tsp ground ginger

Pinch of salt

½ cup (110 g) sweet potato purée

1 cup (250 ml) coconut or nut milk

1–2 tbsp (15–30 ml) maple syrup, optional, or 1–2 tbsp (15–30 ml) coconut milk

1 tsp vanilla extract

¼ cup (30 g) chopped walnuts or pecans

Preheat the oven to 350°F (180°C) and lightly grease a small baking dish (or two large ramekins) with a little melted coconut oil.

In a medium-size bowl, mix the oats, baking powder, cinnamon, nutmeg, cardamom, ginger and salt. Add the purée, milk, syrup and vanilla and mix to combine well.

Spoon the porridge mixture into a dish (or ramekins) and top with chopped walnuts or pecans. Bake for 20 to 25 minutes, depending on the desired consistency (a longer baking time will produce a firmer set).

Let stand for a few minutes to cool slightly, then serve with a little almond milk and/or coconut cream and finish with a sprinkle of extra cinnamon, if you like.

Recipe Notes: To make this nut-free, omit the nuts (replace with pepitas, if you like) and use coconut milk.

To make it oil-free, use nonstick bakeware.

To make it sweetener-free, omit the maple syrup.

Coconut Rice Porridge with Caramelized Banana

Gluten-free | Serves 4-8

Risgrynsgröt, literally "rice grain porridge" in Swedish, is really a pudding of sorts. Though served year round, the dish is still considered by many, including my lovely in-laws, to be strongly connected to the traditional julbord Christmas buffet. My vegan version, complete with additions of coconut and caramelized banana, is far from traditional, but I think the amalgamation of rice and tropical flavors is particularly well matched and thus entirely justifiable! During our most recent Christmas celebration in Sweden, we defied convention and served this version. And my in-laws approved.

⅔ cup (150 g) pudding or short-grain rice

1¼ cups (300 ml) water

¼ tsp salt

2 cups (480 ml) oat or nut milk

1 cup (240 ml) coconut milk + extra for serving, optional

⅓ cup (30 g) unsweetened desiccated coconut

1 cinnamon stick

1 tbsp (9 g) coconut sugar

1 tbsp (15 ml) coconut butter/oil

Caramelized Bananas
2 medium size bananas, sliced into ⅓ inch (8 mm) rounds

2 tsp (6 g) coconut sugar

Pinch of salt

Pinch of pure vanilla powder

1–1½ tbsp (15–22 ml) coconut oil for frying

Ground cardamom for dusting

Toasted coconut flakes for serving, optional

Put the rice, water and salt in a saucepan and bring it to a boil. Cover and reduce the heat to low and let the rice simmer for 10 minutes. Add the nut milk, coconut milk, coconut and the cinnamon stick. Combine well and heat the mixture until hot but not boiling. Cover again and leave the pudding on very low heat until the rice is tender and has absorbed most of the milk. This will normally take between 30 and 45 minutes. Avoid the temptation to stir the rice and keep it covered as much as possible.

While the rice cooks, gently combine the banana slices with the coconut sugar, salt and vanilla powder in a large bowl.

Heat half of the coconut oil in a large skillet/frying pan over medium heat. Space the banana slices out so they are not touching and cook them for about 2 minutes on each side or until caramelized. Transfer the first batch of caramelized bananas to an oven-safe plate. Add a little more oil to the pan, then place more banana slices in it to caramelize. Once all the banana slices are cooked, set the plate to the side until they are needed. They can be warmed through before serving, if you like, in an oven set at 250°F (120°C) for about 10 minutes.

Once the rice is tender and has absorbed most of the milk, remove the pan from the heat and leave it covered for another 10 minutes. Remove the cinnamon stick and stir in the coconut sugar and coconut butter or oil. If the porridge is too thick, stir in a little extra milk.

Serve the porridge in individual portions topped with warm caramelized banana slices and dusted with a pinch of ground cardamom. Top the porridge with extra coconut milk and toasted coconut flakes if you like.

Recipe Note: Fresh mango would work well with this porridge in place of the bananas, if you prefer.

Louie's Baked Santa Porridge (Tomtegröt)

Low-fructose with oil- and nut-free options | Serves 4-6

With less than 1 teaspoon of optional natural sweetener per serving, this sustaining breakfast made from mildly creamy semolina is an easy-to-prep baked porridge and a perfect cold morning treat. Curious recipe name, no? There's a reason for this. In our home, we speak Swenglish; the hybrid mish-mash of Swedish and English that Anglo-Swedish bilingual families such as ours have a tendency to adopt. My son Louie came home from school around Christmas and tried to describe a delicious pudding he'd had which he called Tomtegröt, or Santa Porridge. I was intrigued, and my imagination concocted this recipe based on his Swenglish description. As it turns out, this is not at all reminiscent of what he had that day, but we accidentally stumbled upon a simple light-yet-satisfying, berry-bejeweled breakfast pudding!

---

2 cups + 4 tsp (500 ml) oat or cashew milk

¾ cup (150 g) fine semolina

1 tbsp (9 g) coconut sugar or maple syrup (15 ml), optional

Tiny pinch of salt

1 tsp vanilla extract

Coconut oil or coconut butter for greasing a baking dish

½ cup (50–75 g) or more frozen blackberries, lingonberries and/or blueberries

Preheat the oven to 390°F (200°C).

Heat the milk gently in a large saucepan over medium heat until warm but not simmering.

Add the semolina and sugar (if using) to the milk and stir continuously for about 3 to 5 minutes with a wire whisk until the semolina porridge has thickened well.

Remove the pan from the heat, sprinkle with a tiny pinch of salt and add the vanilla, stirring well to incorporate it. Spoon the mix into a greased baking dish and smooth over the surface with the back of a large metal spoon or a silicone spatula. Sprinkle with the berries and gently press them down into the mix.

Bake the porridge in the oven for 15 to 18 minutes until the berries have thawed and the top of the porridge is a lightly caramelized golden brown color.

Allow to cool slightly before scooping out portions, and serve as is or with coconut cream and/or your favorite milk or a dollop of coconut yogurt.

Recipe Note: To further reduce the fructose, use rice malt syrup in place of coconut sugar or maple syrup.

A Little Sweetness Every Day

Treats, snacks, desserts & puddings

"Hobnots" with Rosemary & Chocolate

Gluten-free with nut-free option | Makes 18-24 cookies

I have always been a fan of the unassuming yet tasty oat-based cookie, or biscuit as I called them growing up in England and Australia. These are a plant-based, low-sweetener twist on one of my favorite tea-time treats from childhood, commonly known by the brand name Hobnobs. My homemade spin on Hobnobs is dressed in a grown-up fashion, with a hint of rosemary and touch of sea salt. Not a fan of dark chocolate? These semi-sweet treats sans chocolate are the perfect accompaniment for vegan cheese on a dairy-free cheese board in place of store-bought crackers.

Cookies

1½ cups (135 g) gluten-free rolled oats

Pinch–¼ tsp dried rosemary, finely chopped

½ cup (60 g) buckwheat flour

½ tsp ground cinnamon

Pinch of salt

2 tbsp (30 ml) maple syrup

⅓ cup (80 ml) coconut oil

3 tbsp (45 ml) coconut or nut milk + extra if needed

Chocolate Coating

⅓ cup (45 g) chopped dark chocolate

½ tsp coconut oil

Sea salt flakes

Preheat the oven to 350°F (180°C). Line a baking sheet with parchment paper.

Tip the oats and rosemary into a food processor and blitz to a coarse flour. Add the buckwheat flour, cinnamon and salt and blitz again to combine. Tip the dry mix into a large mixing bowl. Pour the syrup, oil and milk over the dry ingredients and mix until well combined. If needed, add a little more milk, a teaspoon at a time, to incorporate all ingredients into a workable dough. Form the dough into a large ball with your hands and divide it into halves, reforming each half so that you end up with two separate balls of dough. If your dough is particularly tacky to touch, you can place it in the refrigerator for a few minutes to firm up a little, but not too much or it won't roll without cracking heavily.

Place one of the dough balls onto a piece of parchment paper and roll it out to ⅛ inch (3 mm) in thickness.

With a round cookie cutter approximately 1¾ inches (45 mm) in diameter, cut out circles of cookie dough. Remove the dough off-cuts and add them to the second dough ball.

Place each unbaked cookie on the parchment paper–lined tray you prepared earlier, spacing them about a ⅓ inch (10 mm) apart. Place the baking tray on the center rack of the oven and bake the cookies for about 8 minutes (depending on their size) or until the centers have set and the edges are starting to turn golden brown.

Allow the baked cookies to cool on a wire cooling rack.

Prepare the second tray of cookies by repeating the steps above.

(continued)

"Hobnots" with Rosemary & Chocolate (Continued)

If you have a preferred chocolate melting method, by all means use it, but I prepare the chocolate coating by melting the dark chocolate in a double boiler over low heat.

Add the oil to the melted chocolate and stir well to combine. I'd be remiss not to mention somewhere here that chocolate and water do not play well together, so to avoid it seizing, ensure no water droplets touch your chocolate.

Top each cookie with about a teaspoon of melted chocolate and spread it evenly over the top with a small butter knife, drawing some lines gently through the chocolate with the knife to create ridges, if you like.

When the chocolate has partially set, sprinkle over a modest amount of flaked, crushed sea salt.

Recipe Notes: The chocolate will set fully when cooled, so if the air temperature is warm, pop the cookies in the fridge for a few minutes once coated.

Any remaining cookies can be stored in the fridge for up to 5 days in an airtight container with parchment paper separating cookie layers if needed.

Naturally Sweet Vegan Treats

Chocolate Cutout Sandwich Cookies

Gluten- and grain-free | Makes 60 cookies or 30 sandwich cookies and 1 cup (240 ml) filling

These crisp and chocolaty cutout cookies are perfect for sandwiching together with vanilla cream for a touch of added indulgence and nostalgic charm. Whether you grew up with commercially-produced Oreos or prefer their deliciously raw, whole food counterparts the Raweo, I hope you'll find merit in these cookies, which fall somewhere in the middle of the Oreo-Raweo spectrum. You can easily find the ingredients for the commercial variety by searching online, but I can assure you that the ingredients list for these naturally sweet cookies is, in contrast, a whole-food-lover's delight.

Chocolate Cutout Cookies

2 tbsp (28 g) chia seeds, finely ground + 6 tbsp (90 ml) water

1 cup (100 g) hazelnut meal

1 cup (120 g) almond flour

½ cup (60 g) buckwheat flour

½ tsp ground cinnamon

¼ tsp baking soda

Pinch of salt

⅓ cup + 2 tsp (45 g) raw cacao powder or pure unsweetened cocoa powder

⅓ cup (80 ml) coconut oil, melted

3 tbsp (45 ml) cooked, puréed sweet potato

¼ cup (35 g) coconut sugar

1 tbsp (15 ml) maple syrup

2 tsp (10 ml) vanilla extract

Vanilla Cookie Filling

1 cup (130 g) cashews, soaked overnight

1 tsp vanilla extract

½ tsp pure vanilla powder

2 tsp (10 ml) maple syrup

2 tsp (10 ml) coconut oil

1–2 tbsp (15–30 ml) creamy coconut milk

In a small glass or dish, briskly mix the chia seeds together with the water. Allow the chia mix to sit and jell while you measure the dry ingredients. In a large mixing bowl, combine the hazelnut meal, almond flour, buckwheat flour, cinnamon, baking soda and salt. In a medium-size bowl (or the bowl of a food processor), combine the chia mix with the cacao, oil, sweet potato, sugar, syrup and vanilla. Whisk (or blend) to combine well.

Thoroughly combine the wet and dry mixes to form a dough. Divide the dough into two portions and return them to the mixing bowl. The dough will be sticky, so pop the bowl in the fridge for about 30 minutes if needed to allow the dough to chill and become more workable.

Preheat the oven to 350°F (180°C) and place a sheet of parchment paper on a clean work surface. Place one portion of the chilled dough onto the paper, pat it down slightly with your hand and then place a second sheet of paper on top of it. With a rolling pin, roll the dough out to a thickness of ⅛ inch (3 mm).

For a classic sandwich cookie size, use a round cutter 1¾ inches (45 mm) in diameter. I cut the shapes directly on the parchment paper and remove the off-cuts before sliding the parchment paper onto a baking tray. This is an expeditious way to do things, as these cookies don't spread!

Combine the off-cuts from the first batch of cookies with the remaining dough and repeat the process until all cookies have been made. For this amount of dough, you will probably produce 3 trays worth of cookies, depending upon their size and shape.

Bake the cookies for 8 to 10 minutes, keeping an eye on them to ensure the edges don't darken more than the centers, especially if you've cut out cookie shapes with thin points, such as hearts or stars.

(continued)

Chocolate Cutout Sandwich Cookies (Continued)

Remove the tray from the oven and transfer cookies to a wire rack to cool before frosting.

To make the filling, blitz the cashews, vanilla extract and powder, maple syrup, oil and milk to a smooth and creamy consistency, using an extra tablespoon (15 ml) of coconut milk if necessary to achieve a spreadable texture. To assemble the sandwich cookies, spread about a teaspoon of mix on a cookie and top with a second cookie. Repeat until you have made all of them.

Recipe Note: Reserve any leftover frosting for your next baking venture by storing it in an airtight container in the fridge for up to 5 days or in the freezer for up to 3 months. Allow it to come to a workable temperature and give it a good stir before spreading.

Figgy Squares

Grain- and gluten-free | Makes 16 squares

Tasty and satisfying festive treats, these grain-free bites are packed with deliciously satiating nut protein and jammy fig morsels. Naturally sweetened, each one contains around a third of the amount of sugar (or less) found in many fruit and nut treats on supermarket shelves. Even better, you can make them without adding the host of less wholesome filler ingredients often found in even the healthier store-bought granola bar-style treats. This is a good transition recipe for those who have a sweet tooth and are starting out on the journey to reduce white sugar and processed food consumption.

¾ cup (110 g) blanched almonds

1¼ cups (180 g) cashews

½ cup (45 g) toasted unsweetened desiccated coconut

¼ cup (25 g) almond meal

1 tsp pure vanilla powder

Pinch of salt

⅜ cup (55 g) chopped dried figs

½ tsp arrowroot powder +
1 tbsp (15 ml) water

⅓ cup (80 ml) maple syrup

¼ cup (60 ml) coconut milk

1 tbsp (15 ml) coconut oil

⅓ cup (60 g) dark chocolate, melted (optional)

Preheat the oven to 350°F (180°C). Line a small brownie pan with parchment paper.

Place the almonds and cashews in a single layer on a baking tray lined with parchment paper or foil. Allow them to toast for 5 to 8 minutes (checking them after 4) or until golden brown and fragrant. Remove them from the tray to cool.

Add the nuts to a food processor and pulse a couple of times to chop them. Add the coconut, almond meal, vanilla and salt to the food processor bowl and pulse a couple of times to combine the ingredients.

Tip the mix into a medium- to large-size mixing bowl. Add the chopped figs and stir thoroughly.

Mix the arrowroot powder and water in a small glass to make a slurry. In a small saucepan, bring the arrowroot slurry, syrup, milk and oil to a gentle rolling boil, turn down the heat to medium and allow it to simmer for 2 to 3 minutes, stirring occasionally.

Pour the hot syrup directly over the dry ingredients, using a silicone spatula to scrape the sides of the saucepan to remove all the syrup. Incorporate the wet and dry ingredients, using a spoon to mix.

Tip the mixture into the lined brownie pan and press down firmly. Flatten out the surface evenly with the back of a large metal spoon or silicone spatula.

Bake for 10 minutes. Remove the pan from the oven and allow it to cool completely in the fridge for about 1 to 2 hours. Using a serrated knife, slice the slab into 16 squares.

They are lovely as they are, but if you like, you can dress your squares up with a light drizzle of melted dark chocolate.

soft granola bar
yummy to cream cheeze

Pumpkin Oat Cookies

Gluten-, nut- and oil-free options | Makes approximately 30 cookies

My children cannot get enough of these cookies and my husband, likewise, is a huge fan. So I suppose deeming them fun for all ages is permissible. My family may be unconcerned with the composition of these treats, however, I think the unusually wholesome ingredient combo is one of their most outstanding features. Along with a pleasant, slightly chewy texture and satisfying flavor combo, these cookies are sweetened naturally with 100 percent whole-food ingredients that are easy to source. Secondly, they make a great snack or breakfast on-the-go option. And thirdly, they freeze exceptionally well after baking—if you have some left over to freeze! Bake a batch or two and stock up on deliciously wholesome, grab-and-go treats!

1½ cups (135 g) rolled oats

1 cup (80 g) unsweetened desiccated coconut

4 tbsp (25 g) almond meal or extra oats

1 tsp ground cinnamon

½ tsp ground allspice

½ tsp pure vanilla powder

Pinch of salt

1¼ cups (300 g) mashed ripe banana, packed and leveled (about 2 bananas)

¾ cup (165 g) pure pumpkin purée + a little extra if needed

1 tbsp (15 ml) melted coconut oil or coconut butter

add to dry ingredients ¼ cup (30 g) pecans, finely chopped

¼ cup (45 g) pitted medjool dates, finely chopped

¼ cup (40 g) raisins

Preheat the oven to 350°F (180°C). Line a baking sheet with parchment paper.

Combine the oats, coconut, almond meal, cinnamon, allspice, vanilla and salt in a large mixing bowl. In a medium-size bowl, combine the banana, pumpkin and oil. Pour the wet ingredients over the dry ingredients and stir until well combined. Add the pecans, dates and raisins and fold thoroughly until all the ingredients are incorporated. If the mix seems too dry, add an extra tablespoon or two (15 to 30 ml) of pumpkin purée.

Drop heaped tablespoons (15 ml) of the cookie batter onto the tray, and gently press them down to make evenly shaped circular cookies. Place the tray on the center rack of the oven and bake 16 to 20 minutes (depending on cookie size) or until the middles have set and the edges are golden brown. Remove the cookies from the oven when done and allow them to cool on a wire rack (at least partially) before serving.

Store any remaining cookies in an airtight container in the fridge for up to 5 days or freeze them for up to 3 months (remove them from the freezer 20 minutes before serving).

Recipe Notes: To make these cookies gluten-free, use gluten-free oats.

To make them nut-free, use 4 tablespoons (25 g) of extra oats in place of the almond meal and substitute ¼ cup (35 g) pepitas or sunflower seeds for the pecans.

To make them oil-free, replace the oil in the batter with coconut butter or an extra tablespoon (14 g) of pumpkin purée.

Chocolate Orange Choc-Chip "Box Cake" Cookies

Gluten-free and nut-free options | Makes 20-24 cookies

When cookie meets cake meets chocolate, you know it's going to be good. You've seen them all over Pinterest; delicious looking box cake cookies, made in a flash from commercial cake mix. I'll admit that these take a little more time to whip up, but their taste and satisfyingly soft and slightly cake-like texture mean your efforts will be rewarded with a cookie less ordinary. And knowing exactly what has gone into them ingredient-wise is a bonus too, right?

½ cup (100 g) coconut butter, at room temperature

¼ cup + 2 tbsp (90 ml) olive oil

½ cup (75 g) coconut sugar

⅛ tsp stevia, optional

½ cup + 3 tbsp (165 ml) aquafaba, whisked until slightly thickened and foamy (not whipped)

2 tsp (10 ml) vanilla extract

1 tbsp (15 ml) maple syrup, optional

2 cups (260 g) organic all-purpose flour

¼ cup (25 g) pure unsweetened cocoa powder

1 tsp baking powder

1 tsp baking soda

⅓ tsp salt

¾ cup (110 g) chopped dark chocolate, or chocolate chips

½ cup (60 g) chopped pecans

Zest of an orange, optional (but amazing!)

Preheat the oven to 375°F (190°C). Line two baking trays with parchment paper or spray lightly with oil.

In a large bowl, using electric handheld beaters or the bowl of a stand mixer with a whisk attachment, beat the coconut butter, oil, sugar and stevia (if using) together for about 1 minute.

Add the aquafaba, vanilla and syrup (if using) and beat until well combined. If it looks a little curdled, don't worry. Just continue to whisk until everything is incorporated into a glossy liquid batter.

In a separate large bowl, add the flour, cocoa powder, baking powder, baking soda and salt and mix together. Pour in the liquid mix and stir until completely combined. Fold in the chocolate chips, pecans and zest (if using).

Scoop spoonfuls of the mixture and place them on the tray, flattening them down to make rounds that are ⅕ inch (5 mm) high, and spaced about ½ inch (13 mm) apart or so. They don't spread a lot, so you should have no problem with the cookies running into each other.

Bake the cookies for 7 to 9 minutes. Allow the baked cookies to cool on the baking tray for 5 minutes, and then carefully transfer them to a wire cooling rack to cool completely.

Recipe Notes: To make the cookies nut-free, omit the pecans.

To make the cookies gluten-free, use an all-purpose gluten-free flour blend.

Nutty Crunch Cornflake Cookies

Gluten- and nut-free options | Makes 18 cookies

Looking for a simple baking project? How does two Aussie favorites combined in one easy-to-make semi-sweet treat grab you? I still have occasional cravings for the breakfast cereals I grew up with. One of my childhood favorites, believed for a time to be healthy as it was "made with honey," is actually made with honey in conjunction with three forms of refined sugar and, in fact, just one box of that particular cereal contains a hefty 1¾ cups (350 g) of sugar. Regardless, it was my first introduction to the well-matched flavor combo of peanuts and honey—the flavor of which is replicated here in a vegan-friendly manner through the use of a modest amount of coconut sugar. With these cookies you have an amalgamation of two popular Australian treats: the cornflake cookie and my old favorite nutty, crunchy cornflake cereal. Yet they're far lighter on the sweetener than the muses that inspired them and considerably lower in fat than a traditional cornflake cookie too, if that is of interest!

---

1 tbsp (14 g) chia seeds, finely ground + 5 tbsp (75 ml) water

⅓ cup (80 ml) coconut oil in semi-solid state ideally (non-liquid, but not rock hard)

⅓ cup (50 g) coconut sugar

¼ tsp stevia, optional

1½ tsp (7 g) baking powder

Pinch of salt

1 cup + 2 tbsp (150 g) whole wheat or organic all-purpose flour

2 tbsp (30 ml) almond milk

¼ cup (45 g) chopped roasted peanuts (or dried cranberries/raisins/chopped dates)

1½ cups (45 g) cornflake cereal

Preheat the oven to 350°F (180°C) convection or 375°F (190°C) non-convection. Line a baking tray with parchment paper.

Mix the chia seeds with the water and stir quickly to incorporate well. Let the mix sit for 2 minutes to jell. In a medium-size mixing bowl, combine the oil, sugar, stevia (if using), baking powder, salt and the prepared chia mix. Fold in the flour, add the milk a tablespoon (15 ml) at a time and continue to mix until combined. Fold in the chopped peanuts or dried fruit.

Place the cornflakes in a large bowl and crush them roughly using your hands. Spoon tablespoonfuls (15 ml) of cookie dough into the crushed cornflakes. Toss the mixture gently in the cornflakes to coat and form balls.

Place the balls on the prepared tray, pat them down and space them a ½ inch (13 mm) apart to accommodate for a little spreading. Bake for 14 to 15 minutes or until golden. Remove the tray from the oven and allow the cookies to cool for 10 minutes before transferring to a wire rack to cool completely.

For maximum crunch enjoyment, I recommend eating these on the day of baking, but they will keep stored in an airtight container in the fridge for up to 3 days.

Recipe Notes: Roasted salted peanuts can be used, just skip the pinch of salt if doing so.

To make these cookies gluten-free, use gluten-free all-purpose flour and gluten-free cornflakes.

Naturally Sweet Vegan Treats

Skillet Cookie Pie

Gluten- and nut-free options | Makes 1 (8- to 10-serving) skillet cookie

How do you improve on a chocolate chip cookie? Make it huge and sliceable! Whether you know them as skillet cookies, skillet cookie pies or Pizookies, there's no argument that these pan-baked mega cookies have taken the comfort food world by storm over the past few years. Unlike the common garden-variety skillet cookie, this one is egg-free, lower in fat and far lower in added sweetener of any kind. To make this recipe, I recommend using an 8- to 10-inch (20 to 25 cm) cast iron skillet, but in a pinch a pie dish or brownie pan of the same dimensions can work. A cookie made in a 10-inch (25-cm) skillet will be flatter and take a little less time to bake. A cookie made in an 8-inch (20-cm) skillet will be a little more on the deep-dish side. And remember, a bit gooey in the middle is good, so don't overbake your cookie.

¼ cup (60 ml) aquafaba

⅓ cup (80 ml) coconut oil, melted

⅓ cup (50 g) coconut sugar

3 tbsp (45 ml) smooth hazelnut or seed butter, at room temperature

1 tsp vanilla extract

¾ tsp baking soda

¼ tsp salt

Pinch of stevia, optional

1 cup + 2 tbsp (150 g) organic all-purpose flour

2 tbsp (12 g) almond or oat flour

½ cup (65 g) dark chocolate, chopped (or dark chocolate chips)

½ cup (65 g) walnuts, pecans or hazelnuts, chopped

Dairy-free ice cream, Coconut Whip (page 183) or Coconut Milk Chocolate Ganache (page 72), to serve, optional

Preheat the oven to 325°F (165°C).

In a large mixing bowl or the bowl of a stand mixer with a paddle attachment, whisk the aquafaba until it is foamy and slightly thickened, but not completely whipped. Add the oil, sugar, nut butter and vanilla to the bowl. Mix well, either by hand or on medium speed in a stand mixer.

Add the baking soda, salt and stevia (if using). Combine well. The mix should have a glossy finish. Add the all-purpose flour and the almond flour, folding the flours thoroughly to incorporate with the wet mix. Add the chocolate and nuts and fold in thoroughly to incorporate.

Press the mix into an ungreased skillet pan, smoothing out the surface with the back of a large metal spoon or silicone spatula. Bake the skillet cookie for 15 to 20 minutes or until the edges are set and lightly golden brown. Don't worry if the center is slightly gooey, and note that the cookie will firm upon cooling too.

Allow the cookie to cool for at least a few minutes before slicing and serving. The skillet will be hot. To serve, slice and top with your optional toppings or eat it just as it is!

Recipe Notes: For a gluten-free cookie, use a combination of 1 cup + 2 tablespoons (150 g) gluten-free all-purpose flour and 2 tablespoons (12 g) of almond flour.

For a nut-free cookie, use seed butter, oat flour instead of almond and omit the chopped nuts (adding more chocolate instead, if you like).

Lillian's Lemon Scones

No added unrefined sweetener option | Makes 16-18 small scones

Near and dear to my heart, a version of these dainty, date-sweetened, fragrantly lemony scones were made just hours before my daughter Lillian was born. In fact, I was in active labor as I embarked upon a last-minute, hormonally-fueled scone-baking frenzy. Strangely, it is one of my fondest memories—not only of my pregnancy, but also of my life. That night, I hovered between watching clips of MasterChef Australia, my comfort viewing of choice at the time, and MasterChef MasterClass, where chef Gary Mehigan's date and lemon scones piqued my pregnancy-driven cravings. I baked, pausing every couple of minutes to breathe through a contraction, and at around 9 pm, I inexplicably invited family members over for fika. They humored me and came. Around midnight, all carbed up on scones, I headed to the hospital in an oddly serene frame of mind. Less than 4 hours later, our little miracle entered the world. Scones, and Lillian's delightful lemon scones in particular, will have a special place in my heart forever more.

⅔ cup (160 ml) full-fat coconut milk + a little extra for brushing over

3 tbsp (45 ml) plant yogurt of choice (oat works well)

3 cups (360 g) spelt flour

4 tsp (18 g) baking powder

¼ tsp salt

⅓ cup (80 ml) coconut butter, stirred and at room temperature

1 cup (180 g) pitted medjool dates

Zest of 1–2 lemons (according to taste preference), finely grated

A small amount of coconut sugar for dusting, optional

Pear + Blackberry Jam with Agar-Agar (page 188), Basic Strawberry Chia Jam (191) or Coconut Whip (page 183), to serve, optional

Preheat the oven to 390°F (200°C). Line a flat baking tray with parchment paper.

Whisk the milk and yogurt together in a medium-size mixing bowl.

In a large bowl, combine the flour, baking powder and salt, mixing them together with a fork before pouring in the coconut butter. Cut the coconut butter through the flour mix using the fork, and then use your fingertips to break up the larger clumps into crumbs.

Chop the dates into small pieces (no bigger than the size of a raisin) and add them together with the lemon zest to the flour mix. Use your fingertips to incorporate the sticky date pieces evenly throughout the flour. Pour in the milk mixture and stir gently to bring all the ingredients to a soft dough, adding a little extra milk if necessary. Turn the dough onto a lightly floured surface and knead gently until it comes together. If the dough is too sticky to work with, add a little extra flour.

Press the dough out to a roughly rectangular form ⅘ inch (20 mm) thick. Use a 2¼-inch (57-mm) diameter cutter or a small glass to cut scones from the dough and place them onto the prepared tray flat-side up to create an even surface texture on the tops of your scones. Press the remaining dough off-cuts together gently and repeat the process of cutting out scones to use up the remaining dough. Space the scones evenly on the tray. It is not necessary to leave more than ⅔ inch (17 mm) between them as they will not spread.

(continued)

Naturally Sweet Vegan Treats

Lillian's Lemon Scones (Continued)

Brush the scone tops with coconut milk and, if you like, sprinkle with a little coconut sugar.

Bake the scones for 10 to 12 minutes or until golden, risen and baked through. Remove the tray from the oven and allow the scones to cool slightly on a wire cooling rack before serving.

Serve the scones warm or cold as they are, or with jam and Coconut Whip, if you like.

Recipe Note: To make the scones free from added unrefined sweeteners, omit the sprinkle of coconut sugar before you bake the scones.

Baked "Buttermilk" Doughnuts with Maple Pecan Frosting

Oil-, gluten- and nut-free options | Makes 10-12 small doughnuts and $^1/_2$ cup (120 ml) frosting

As artisan "doughnutteries" pop up in all the hipster hubs around the globe selling ever more outlandish and Instagramable doughnut concoctions, I do believe there is still a place for a humbler and less neon-hued or sugar-drenched homemade version. Enter these baked "buttermilk" doughnuts. Thanks to a combination of apple cider vinegar, lemon juice and plant milk, not only is the flavor of buttermilk replicated, but the effect of buttermilk is as well. Thus these doughnuts are kept moist and tender as the slightly acidic batter helps to break down the long strands of gluten in the flour. This batter produces a rather light, subtly sweet and neutral baked doughnut that can be frosted in any way you please! I do, however, recommend the maple pecan frosting because it's been my personal favorite over the past few years. Chocolate glaze in the form of From-Scratch Basic Chocolate Ganache (page 196) or Chocolate & Peanut Butter Fudge Topping (page 195) or a light dusting of cinnamon coconut sugar would also be lovely.

"Buttermilk" Doughnuts

¾ cup (180 ml) nut or oat milk

1½ tsp (8 ml) apple cider vinegar

1½ tsp (8 ml) lemon juice

½ tsp vanilla extract

1¾ cups (210 g) spelt or (230 g) organic all-purpose flour

2 tbsp (6 g) cornstarch

2 tsp (9 g) baking powder

¼–½ tsp salt

⅓ cup (50 g) coconut sugar

⅛ tsp pure powdered stevia, optional

1 tsp ground cinnamon

¼ tsp ground nutmeg, optional

½ cup (120 ml) unsweetened applesauce

2 tbsp (30 ml) coconut oil, melted (or 2 tbsp [30 ml] extra applesauce)

Preheat the oven to 425°F (220°C). If using a silicone baking form, no greasing is required. If using a doughnut pan, prepare it by lightly greasing with melted coconut oil or olive oil.

In a small bowl, combine the milk, vinegar, lemon juice and vanilla. Into a large bowl, sift the flour, cornstarch, baking powder and salt. Add the coconut sugar, stevia (if using), cinnamon and nutmeg (if using) to the dry ingredients and whisk together.

Add the milk mixture, applesauce and coconut oil (or extra applesauce) to the dry mix. Fold until just combined. Allow the batter to sit for 5 minutes for the baking powder to activate.

Fill each doughnut cup approximately three-quarters full. Bake for 7 to 9 minutes or until the doughnuts are cooked through and their tops spring back when touched.

Allow the doughnuts to cool for 5 minutes before removing them from the pan. Carefully ease them out to prevent cracking. Transfer the doughnuts to a wire cooling rack to cool completely before frosting.

(continued)

Baked "Buttermilk" Doughnuts with Maple Pecan Frosting (Continued)

Maple Pecan Frosting

⅓ cup + 2 tbsp (60 g) pecans

2 tbsp (30 ml) maple syrup

2 tbsp (30 ml) coconut oil, melted

2–3 tbsp (30–45 ml) warm water

Pinch of ground cinnamon

Pinch of sea salt

To make the frosting, blitz the pecans, syrup, oil, water, cinnamon and salt in a small food processor or blender until smooth, adding a tablespoon (15 ml) of extra water if needed to achieve the desired consistency.

Recipe Notes: To make the doughnuts oil-free, use a silicone baking mold and 2 extra tablespoons (30 ml) of applesauce in place of the coconut oil.

To make the doughnuts and frosting nut-free, use oat instead of nut milk and top with Coconut Milk Chocolate Ganache (page 72) or Easy Avocado Chocolate Whip (page 196) instead of the Maple Pecan Frosting.

To make the doughnuts gluten-free, use a gluten-free all-purpose flour blend in place of spelt or organic all-purpose flour.

Double Choc Doughnuts

Gluten-free with an oil-free option | Makes 10-12 small doughnuts and 1¹/₄ cups (300 ml) ganache

What's better than chocolate? A double dose of chocolate, of course. I am not a fan of using the term "guilt-free" to describe recipes. Partly because I think it is often confused with the term "free-from" (as in, allergy-friendly), and partly because I don't like the idea of associating eating with experiencing shame. In any case, if you do happen to prefer or need to eat grain-free, gluten-free or oil-free, this is a recipe that might tick boxes for you. And if you like chocolate, well, you're definitely in luck!

Chocolate Doughnuts

¾ cup (180 ml) nut or oat milk

1 tbsp (15 ml) apple cider vinegar

1 tsp vanilla extract

¼ cup (25 g) pure unsweetened cocoa powder

¾ cup + 1 tbsp (100 g) buckwheat flour

¾ cup + 1 tbsp (80 g) almond flour

2 tbsp (18 g) cornstarch or arrowroot powder

2 tsp (9 g) baking powder

½–¾ tsp salt

¼–⅓ cup (35–50 g) coconut sugar

½ cup (120 g) mashed ripe banana, packed and leveled

2 tbsp (30 ml) coconut oil, melted (or 2 tbsp [30 g] extra mashed banana)

Coconut Milk Chocolate Ganache

¼ cup (60 ml) unsweetened coconut cream

Tiny pinch of salt

1 cup (150 g) chopped dairy-free dark chocolate

Preheat the oven to 425°F (220°C). If using a silicone baking form, no greasing is required. If using a doughnut pan, prepare it by lightly greasing it with a little melted coconut oil or olive oil.

In a small bowl, combine the milk, vinegar and vanilla.

Into a large bowl, sift together the cocoa powder, buckwheat and almond flour, cornstarch, baking powder and salt. Add the coconut sugar and whisk together.

Add the milk mixture, banana and oil (or extra mashed banana) to the dry mix and fold in until just combined. If using arrowroot powder instead of cornstarch, allow the mix to sit for 15 minutes to give the arrowroot time to hydrate.

Fill each doughnut cup approximately three-quarters full. Bake for 7 to 9 minutes or until the doughnut tops spring back when touched. Allow the doughnuts to cool for 5 minutes before removing them from the pan. Carefully ease them out to prevent cracking. Transfer the doughnuts to a wire cooling rack to cool completely before frosting.

To make the ganache, add the cream and a tiny pinch of salt to a small saucepan. Place it over low-medium heat and bring it to the gentlest simmer to heat through. Do not allow it to boil. Pop the chocolate in a medium-large ceramic or glass bowl, pour the hot coconut milk over it and let it sit until the chocolate is soft, about 5 minutes. Use a silicone spatula or spoon to very gently fold the mixture until the ganache is smooth and shiny. If it splits, pop the bowl over a hot water bath and add 2 tablespoons (30 ml) of coconut cream. Stir gently to bring the ganache together.

Recipe Note: To make these doughnuts oil-free, use a silicone baking mold and 2 extra tablespoons (30 g) of mashed banana in place of the coconut oil.

Very Veggie Cupcakes with Coconut Whip

Nut-, gluten- and fructose-free options | Makes 18-24 cupcakes

For those who never imagined cupcakes could contribute to your "five a day," allow me to introduce this muffin-cupcake hybrid boasting up to 3 servings of vegetables plus optional coconut frosting (to increase the cupcake credibility factor). I don't make a point of sneaking vegetables into the food of my little ones, but it is a useful trick to have up your sleeve.

2½ cups (300 g) spelt or organic all-purpose flour

1 tsp baking powder

2 tsp (10 g) baking soda

1½ tsp (4 g) ground cinnamon

Pinch of ground nutmeg

Pinch of ground ginger

¼ tsp salt

1 cup + 1 tbsp (255 g) sweet potato purée (or mashed ripe banana), packed and leveled

⅓ cup + 2 tbsp (110 ml) maple syrup

1 tsp apple cider vinegar

¼ cup (60 ml) coconut oil or coconut butter, melted

1 cup (110 g) grated carrot

¾ cup (115 g) grated zucchini

⅓ cup (40 g) walnuts, chopped

Coconut Whip (page 183)

Cinnamon to sprinkle, optional

Preheat the oven to 325°F (160°C) convection or 345°F (175°C) non-convection. In a large bowl, mix the flour, baking powder, baking soda, cinnamon, nutmeg, ginger and salt. In a medium-size mixing bowl, combine the sweet potato, syrup, vinegar, oil, carrot and zucchini and incorporate well. Tip the wet mix over the dry mix and fold gently to incorporate. Add the walnuts and gently fold through.

Scoop the batter into 18 to 24 cupcake liners (depending on desired size), filling each liner to three-quarter capacity. Bake for 25 to 30 minutes or until a toothpick inserted in the center comes out clean. Eat these cupcakes warm as they are, or allow them to cool and frost them with Coconut Whip, either by spreading or by piping. Finish the cupcakes with a sprinkle of cinnamon, if you like.

Recipe Notes: To make the cupcakes gluten-free, replace the spelt or all-purpose flour with a gluten-free flour blend.

To make the cupcakes nut-free, omit the walnuts and replace them with ¼ cup (35 g) of sunflower seeds.

To make the cupcakes fructose-free, replace the maple syrup with ⅓ cup + 1 tbsp (95 ml) of rice malt syrup plus 1 tbsp (15 ml) of water.

Oliver's Chewy Blueberry Granola Bars

Nut-free, no added unrefined sweetener with gluten-free option | Makes 8-16 pieces

The perfect subtly sweet treat for tiny tots and busy grown-ups! When our littlest family member Oliver decided to completely bypass the mushy baby food stage and headed directly from milk to solids, wholesome homemade treats were just the ticket. These bars are sweetened only with fruit and berries, but not overly so. And being lactose-, egg- and nut-free with a gluten-free option, they may also provide a perfect easy-to-assemble, allergy-friendly contribution to kids' parties, school lunch boxes and picnics.

---

2 cups (180 g) rolled oats, gluten-free, if preferred

1½ tbsp (9 g) unsweetened desiccated coconut, optional (but recommended)

1 tsp ground cinnamon

½ cup (75 g) fresh or frozen blueberries (frozen will turn the bars purple)

⅓ cup (50 g) dried currants

¼ cup (60 ml) coconut oil or coconut butter, melted

¼ cup (60 g) mashed ripe banana, packed and leveled

¼ cup (60 ml) unsweetened applesauce at room temperature

⅓ cup (80 ml) + 1–2 tbsp (15–30 ml) plant yogurt (oat, soy or almond) at room temperature

Preheat the oven to 330°F (165°C) and line a brownie pan with parchment paper.

Blitz the oats, coconut (if using) and cinnamon in a food processor to produce a coarse crumb texture. Transfer the mix to a large bowl and add the blueberries and currants.

To the bowl of a food processor, add the oil, banana, applesauce and yogurt and whizz until well combined.

Add the wet mix to the oat mix and stir to incorporate. If the mix seems a little too dry or crumbly, add an extra 1 to 2 tablespoons (15 to 30 ml) of yogurt to help bring it together. Scoop the mixture into the prepared pan and press down with the back of the spoon to make it compact and smooth.

Bake for 20 to 25 minutes or until the edges begin to turn golden brown.

Allow the slab to cool for 15 minutes. Carefully lift the parchment paper edges to remove the granola bar slab from the pan, and allow it to cool completely on a wire rack or in the fridge before cutting into bars or squares.

Recipe Notes: To make these bars gluten-free, use gluten-free oats.

These granola bars can be stored in an airtight container in the fridge for up to 3 days or frozen for up to 3 months. Remove them from the freezer at least 40 minutes before serving.

Veggie Patch Brownies

Oil-free with nut- and gluten-free options | Makes 12-16 brownies

Delightfully fudgy and chocolaty, these brownies pack a stealthy and surprising veggie punch. I admit that I don't ordinarily sneak vegetables into dishes, but if there's an opportunity to bake something that's not only delicious but also a little more wholesome, why not take it? These brownies are lovely just as they are, and veggie fussy children and adults are highly unlikely to spot the inclusion of vegetables let alone the absence of dairy and eggs. What's more, these brownies are definitely lighter on sugar than traditional ones. Please note that I use unsweetened cocoa powder in this recipe as opposed to raw cacao, as I personally prefer the way the flavors balance in this instance. Frosting is entirely optional, but I heartily recommend the Fudge Frosting (page 139) and Brownie Batter Fudge Butter (page 184), if you are keen!

½ cup (100 g) sweet potato purée

½ cup (75 g) grated zucchini, excess liquid squeezed out

1 cup (240 ml) almond milk or oat milk

⅓ cup (50 g) coconut sugar

8 pitted medjool dates, soaked in boiled water for 10 minutes

1½ tsp (8 ml) pure vanilla extract

¾ cup (100 g) organic whole wheat pastry flour

¾ cup (75 g) pure unsweetened cocoa powder

1 tsp baking powder

Pinch of salt

½ cup (60 g) chopped walnuts

¼ cup (37 g) chopped dark chocolate, optional (but recommended)

Preheat the oven to 350°F (180°C). Line a 9 × 9 inch (23 × 23 cm) square cake pan with parchment paper.

Blitz the sweet potato, zucchini, milk, sugar, drained dates and vanilla together in a food processor or blender until the mix is a smooth, soup-like consistency. Tip this mixture into a large mixing bowl. Sift in the flour, cocoa powder, baking powder and salt. Gently fold to combine. Add the walnuts and chocolate (if using). Fold in, but do not overmix.

Pour the brownie batter into the lined pan and smooth over the surface with a silicone spatula or the back of a large metal spoon. Place on the center rack of the oven and bake for 20 to 25 minutes.

Allow to cool completely before frosting, if desired. Slice into squares to serve.

Recipe Notes: To make these brownies nut-free, use oat milk and omit the walnuts. If frosting the brownies, choose a nut-free frosting option such as the Love Yummies frosting (page 119).

To make the brownies gluten-free, use a gluten-free all-purpose flour and baking powder.

Butter Bean Blondies, Two Ways

Oil-free with gluten-free option | Makes 12-16 blondies

White Chocolate Macadamia or Spiced Apple Pie? The choice is yours. Subtle in flavor, pleasantly fudgy in texture and easy on the sweetness, the White Chocolate Macadamia Blondies are a great semi-sweet option for those who don't like a super-rich chocolate brownie. Oliver and Lillian, my two youngest children, in particular like these. And my hubby, who was raised on Swedish cinnamon buns (kanelbullar), thoroughly enjoys the Spiced Apple Pie Blondies—a blondie-meets-slice-of-apple-pie hybrid—with a cup of tea, finding they're just the right combo of a little sweetness and warming spice in a post-meal treat.

White Chocolate Macadamia Blondies

¾ cup (65 g) rolled oats

¾ cup (75 g) almond flour

1 tsp baking powder

Pinch of salt

1 cup (200 g) cooked/canned white beans

½ cup (130 g) unsweetened applesauce

3 tbsp (45 ml) maple syrup

3 tbsp (45 ml) coconut milk

2½ tsp (12 ml) vanilla extract

⅓ cup (50 g) chopped vegan white chocolate

⅓ cup (50 g) roughly chopped lightly roasted macadamia nuts

To make either version, preheat the oven to 350°F (180°C). Line a brownie pan with parchment paper.

To make the White Chocolate Macadamia Nut Blondies, pulse the oats in a food processor to make a coarse flour. Combine the oats with the flour, baking powder and salt in a large mixing bowl.

Blitz the beans, applesauce, syrup, milk and vanilla in a food processor and add them to the dry mix, stirring to incorporate. Add the white chocolate plus macadamias and fold together. Spoon the batter into the brownie pan, smoothing over the surface with a silicone spatula or the back of a spoon.

(continued)

Spiced Apple Pie Blondies

¾ cup (65 g) rolled oats

¾ cup (75 g) hazelnut meal

1 tsp baking powder

2 tsp (5 g) ground cinnamon

1 tsp ground cardamom

Pinch of ground allspice

Pinch of salt

1 cup + 1 tbsp (200 g) cooked/canned white beans

½ cup (130 g) unsweetened applesauce

3 tbsp (45 ml) maple syrup

3 tbsp (45 ml) coconut milk

2 tsp (10 ml) vanilla extract

⅓ cup (50 g) raisins

⅓ cup (65 g) grated fresh apple, packed

To make the Spiced Apple Pie Blondies, pulse the oats in a food processor to make a coarse flour. Combine the oats with the hazelnut meal, baking powder, cinnamon, cardamom, allspice and salt in a large mixing bowl.

Blitz the beans, applesauce, syrup, milk and vanilla in a food processor and add to the dry mix, stirring to incorporate. Add the raisins plus apple and fold through. Spoon the batter into the brownie pan, smoothing over the surface with a silicone spatula or the back of a spoon.

Bake the blondies to your liking for between 20 to 24 minutes or until a toothpick inserted in the center comes out mostly clean. A shorter baking time will produce a gooier consistency and a longer one will produce a more set, cake-like texture.

Remove the blondies from the oven and leave to cool for at least 20 minutes before carefully removing the slab from the pan and slicing it into squares.

These blondies are great enjoyed straight after baking (after the slight cooling time), or warmed up later on.

Though further additions are unneeded, these blondies can also be cooled completely and frosted with Basic Vanilla Cream Frosting (page 180).

Store any uneaten blondies in an airtight container in the fridge for up to 5 days or in the freezer for up to 3 months.

Recipe Note: To make these blondies gluten-free, use gluten-free oats.

Nectarine & Strawberry Galettes

Gluten-free with oil-free option | Makes 4 individual galettes

The charmingly rustic and slightly show-off-y galette is surely the free-form darling of the pie world or, as I have seen it put, "pie's perfectly imperfect cousin." And what better way to showcase the bounty of summer than by allowing the natural sweetness of fresh strawberries and lush nectarines to shine from a frame of pretty pastry. Frangipane and stone fruit are a perfect paring, but add strawberries and pastry and you have a next level summery pie combo.

Pastry

2 tbsp (28 g) chia or flax seeds, finely ground + 6 tbsp (90 ml) water

1½ cups (200 g) buckwheat flour, packed and leveled

1½ cups (150 g) almond flour

1 tbsp (9 g) cornstarch

1½ tbsp (14 g) coconut sugar

Pinch of salt

3 tbsp (45 ml) coconut oil or coconut butter

2–3 tbsp (30–45 ml) water at room temperature

Frangipane Pastry Cream

¾ cup (75 g) almond flour

¼ tsp ground cinnamon

3½ tbsp (53 ml) coconut milk + extra for brushing pastry

1 tbsp (9 g) coconut sugar + 2–4 tsp (6–12 g) extra for sprinkling over

Preheat the oven to 350°F (180°C).

Mix the chia seeds with the water. Stir quickly to incorporate well and let the mix sit for a couple of minutes.

Combine the buckwheat flour, almond flour, cornstarch, sugar and salt in a food processor/blender and pulse them to combine. Add the coconut oil and pulse again until a crumb-like texture is achieved. Add the chia mix along with 2 tablespoons (30 ml) of water and pulse until the dough comes together, adding an extra tablespoon (15 ml) of water if needed.

Divide the pastry into 4 portions of equal size, roll each one into a ball and refrigerate while you prepare the pastry cream.

Make the frangipane pastry cream filling by combining the almond flour, cinnamon, coconut milk and 1 tablespoon (9 g) of coconut sugar in a medium-size bowl.

Prepare the filling in a separate medium-size bowl. Drizzle the sliced nectarines and strawberries with the maple syrup and sprinkle with the nutmeg.

Roll out each ball of pastry between two sheets of parchment paper into a circle of a uniform ⅛ inch (3 mm) thickness, approximately 7 inches (18 cm) in diameter. If you find the dough too sticky to work with, you can refrigerate the dough a little longer, but do note that longer periods of refrigeration may solidify the pastry too much for it to be immediately workable (as a result of the way coconut oil behaves).

(continued)

Nectarine & Strawberry Galettes (Continued)

Filling

2–3 nectarines, pitted and sliced

1 cup (155 g) hulled and halved strawberries (quartered if large)

1 tbsp (15 ml) maple syrup

Pinch of ground nutmeg

Spread an equal amount of pastry cream (a little over a tablespoon [15 ml]) around the center of each of your 4 pastry rounds.

Divide the fruit among each pastry circle and arrange as you like, reserving the leftover syrup for serving later.

Gently pinch and fold the edges of the pastry of each galette to create a border with a width of an inch (25 mm), then brush the pastry with a little coconut cream. Sprinkle each galette (both the pastry border and fruit) with a ½ teaspoon to 1 teaspoon of coconut sugar.

Bake the galettes for 20 minutes or until the pastry is crisp golden brown.

Allow the galettes to cool slightly before serving, drizzled with the remaining syrup from earlier and, by all means, with a scoop of nice-cream!

Recipe Note: To make these galettes oil-free, use coconut butter in place of coconut oil. Make sure to stir the butter well before measuring.

Whole Wheat Banana & Walnut Bread

Oil-free with nut-free option | Makes 1 loaf

A make-ahead and easily frozen classic and a crowd pleaser, this recipe in some variation or another has been a family favorite for years. Over time I have reduced the amount of sugar significantly, allowing the natural sweetness of the banana to shine through while the texture remains more or less unchanged. Wonderful as a snack, for afternoon tea, breakfast, brunch or even dessert, this delicious bread also freezes and defrosts beautifully! It's quite possibly the perfect make-ahead treat.

---

2 cups (260 g) organic whole-wheat pastry flour or organic all-purpose flour

⅓ cup (50 g) coconut sugar

¾ tsp baking soda

¼ tsp salt

2 tsp (5 g) ground cinnamon

1 tsp pure vanilla powder

½ cup (120 ml) cashew milk or other non-dairy milk of choice

1½ tsp (8 ml) organic apple cider vinegar

1⅓ cups (320 g) mashed ripe banana, packed and leveled

½ cup (65 g) organic walnuts, roughly chopped

Preheat the oven to 350°F (180°C). Grease and line a loaf pan with parchment paper.

In a large bowl, combine the flour, sugar, baking soda, salt, cinnamon and vanilla. In a small bowl, combine the milk and vinegar. Add the milk and vinegar combination to the dry ingredients, followed by the bananas. Fold gently to combine. Add the walnuts and fold them gently through until incorporated, but do not overmix. Pour the batter into the lined loaf pan and bake the bread for 45 to 50 minutes, or until a toothpick inserted in the center comes out clean.

Remove the bread from the oven and allow it to cool for at least 20 minutes on a wire cooling rack to aid in easier slicing.

Recipe Notes: To make this bread nut-free, replace the walnuts with ⅓ cup (45 g) of sunflower seeds.

To freeze for later use, allow the bread to cool completely, then place it in a resealable freezer bag to freeze. Alternatively, slice the loaf and place the individual slices in an airtight container to store in the freezer, ready to take out a slice at a time as required.

To warm the frozen slices for serving, microwave individual frozen slices of banana bread for 20 seconds or so, or toast and warm them through in a non-stick skillet pan.

Naturally Sweet Vegan Treats

Blueberry Muffin Mug Cakes

No added unrefined sweetener, gluten- and grain-free
with nut-free option | Makes 2 servings

A warm cake with a tender crumb, speckled with nuts and berries, that's baked and ready to eat in 1 minute and 30 seconds? You bet! Otherwise known as muggins, these magical mini treats can be enjoyed straight from the mug just minutes after you decide that dessert is in order. No fuss, no added sweetener, no big clean-up operation. Blueberry Muffin Mug Cakes are a beneficial balance of wholesome, whole-food ingredients and minimal effort in individual treat form.

---

1 tbsp (15 ml) melted coconut oil + a little extra for greasing, divided

⅓ cup (40 g) buckwheat flour

½ tsp baking powder

⅛ tsp baking soda

Pinch of salt

Pinch of ground nutmeg

½ tsp ground cinnamon

⅓ cup (120 g) mashed ripe banana (1 medium banana)

⅓ cup (80 ml) almond milk

½ tsp vanilla extract

2 tbsp (20 g) chopped walnuts + extra for topping if desired

2 tbsp (40 g) dried or fresh blueberries + extra for topping if desired

Lightly grease the insides of two microwave-safe mugs with a little melted coconut oil. In a medium-size mixing bowl (ideally with a lip for ease of pouring), mix the flour, baking powder, baking soda, salt, nutmeg, cinnamon, banana, milk, oil and vanilla. Add the walnuts and blueberries and fold together. Pour the cake batter into the mugs. Top with an extra sprinkle of chopped walnuts or blueberries, if desired.

Cook each mug cake in the microwave on high (900 watt) for 1 minute and 30 seconds, turning the mugs halfway through the cooking time if your microwave doesn't have a turntable.

If the cake is not cooked to your liking, pop it back in the microwave for 5 to 10 seconds.

If you don't have a microwave or prefer not to use one, simply use oven-safe mugs or large individual ramekins and bake the cakes in an oven at 350°F (180°C) for 20 minutes.

Recipe Note: To make these mug cakes nut-free, omit the walnuts and replace the almond milk with oat or coconut milk.

Autumnal Parsnip, Apple & Ginger Cake

Makes 1 (9-inch [23-cm]) cake

As the days shorten and become increasingly chilly, this cozy and thoroughly unfussy cake, infused with the flavors of the season, is an agreeably warming way to celebrate the transition into colder months. For the past few years, we've welcomed the autumn and winter seasons with fika featuring variations of parsnip and apple cake. Over time it has transformed into something lighter and far less sweet—my first versions were positively slathered with sweetened cream cheese frosting. A hint of warming fresh ginger gives this humble, rustic cake a seasonally apt flavor boost.

1½ cups (190 g) organic all-purpose flour

1 tbsp (3 g) cornstarch

1 tbsp (9 g) coconut sugar

½ tsp baking powder

1 tsp baking soda

Pinch of salt

2 tsp (5 g) ground cinnamon

¼ tsp ground cloves

½ cup (95 g) grated apple, packed

½ cup (70 g) grated parsnip, packed

½ cup (55 g) chopped pecans

2 tsp (12 g) grated fresh ginger (or more to taste)

½ cup (120 ml) hot water

½ cup (120 ml) olive oil + a little extra for greasing

¼ cup (60 ml) maple syrup

2 tsp (10 ml) vanilla extract

2 tsp (10 ml) apple cider vinegar

1–2 tbsp (7–14 g) coconut flour for dusting, optional

Preheat the oven to 350°F (180°C). Prepare a round 9-inch (23-cm) cake pan by greasing it lightly and lining the base with parchment paper.

In a large mixing bowl, combine the flour, cornstarch, sugar, baking powder, baking soda, salt, cinnamon and cloves until well incorporated. Add in the apple, parsnip, pecans and fresh ginger. Fold the ingredients thoroughly. In a separate smaller mixing bowl, combine the water, oil, syrup, vanilla and vinegar. Pour the wet mix over the dry mix and fold through until all ingredients are incorporated.

Pour the batter into the prepared cake pan and bake for 25 to 30 minutes or until a toothpick inserted in the center comes out clean.

Allow the cake to cool in the pan for 15 minutes before carefully removing it and transferring it to a wire cooling rack to cool completely.

Once cooled and ready to serve, dust it lightly with coconut flour.

Naturally Sweet Vegan Treats

Pumpkin & Candied Pecan Hand Pies

Makes 6 hand pies

Made from scratch with Olive Oil Short Crust Pastry or with time-crunch-friendly store-bought vegan puff pastry, these pumpkin-packed treats positively exude autumn. If candied pecans, puréed pumpkin and aromatic sweet spices encased in a pastry pocket that's baked until crisp doesn't scream fall, I don't know what does. And all this coziness is brought to you with less than 1 teaspoon of added natural sweetener per hand pie.

---

1 quantity of Olive Oil Short Crust Pastry (page 175)

⅓ cup (35 g) pecans, chopped

1 tsp melted coconut oil

1 tbsp (15 ml) maple syrup

⅓ cup + 1 tbsp (95 g) pumpkin purée (canned or homemade), packed and leveled

¾ tbsp (7 g) coconut sugar + extra for sprinkling

½ tsp ground cinnamon

¼ tsp ground ginger

Pinch of ground allspice

Pinch of ground nutmeg

Pinch of salt

Pinch of pure vanilla powder

Water for brushing the pastry

Coconut milk for brushing the pastry

Prepare the pastry as directed and set aside.

In a skillet/frying pan over medium heat, add the pecans, coconut oil and maple syrup. Allow the nuts to toast for 3 minutes, stirring occasionally. Remove the pan from the heat, tip the nuts into a bowl and set to the side to cool.

Preheat the oven to 350°F (180°C).

In a small mixing bowl, combine the pumpkin, sugar, cinnamon, ginger, allspice, nutmeg, salt and vanilla. Add the cooled candied pecans and fold through.

Roll out the pastry and cut it into six 5-inch (12-cm) rounds using a cutter or a bowl of that approximate size as a guide to cut around with a small, sharp knife. Spoon about 1¾ tablespoons (19 g) of pumpkin filling onto the center of each pastry circle.

Brush the edges of each pastry circle with a little water. Carefully fold the pastry over the filling to create a half moon shape and press the edges to seal. Crimp the edges of each hand pie with a fork, pushing the tines down. Using a small, sharp knife, cut three small slits in the tops of the pies.

Carefully slide the parchment paper with the pies onto a flat baking tray. Brush the tops of the pies with coconut milk and sprinkle them with a little coconut sugar. Place the tray on the center rack of the oven and bake the pies for about 18 minutes or until they are golden brown.

Let the pies cool on the baking tray (placed on a wire rack) for at least 15 minutes before serving.

Recipe Note: Store-bought vegan puff pastry can be used in place of pastry made from scratch. Simply follow the filling directions and assembly steps as detailed above, but skip brushing the pies with coconut milk or sprinkling with coconut sugar.

Pear & Cardamom Pudding

Gluten- and grain-free, low-oil, low-sweetener | Makes about 8 servings

Would you believe me if I told you this grain-, gluten-, dairy- and egg-free, low-sweetener pudding was inspired by the comfort classic, clafoutis? Yes, it's true (staunch clafoutis traditionalists, please avert your eyes!), but as will be immediately evident to anyone who knows clafoutis, this pudding is actually entirely dissimilar. I used to make a traditional version of clafoutis for my friends and family and, for a time during his pre-vegan days, my husband deemed it a favorite homemade treat. So, for his birthday, I decided to get a little creative and this was the result. It may be nothing like the dish that inspired it, however, if you have to (or choose to) avoid certain ingredients, this is a comforting pudding alternative that's sure to please your tummy and make your kitchen smell delightful on a cozy autumn afternoon.

---

2 tbsp (28 g) chia seeds, finely ground + ½ cup (120 ml) water

½ cup + 1 tsp (125 ml) almond milk

1 tbsp olive oil (15 ml) + extra for greasing

2 tbsp (15 ml) maple syrup

½ cup (50 g) almond flour

½ cup (60 g) hazelnut meal

1½ tsp (7 g) baking powder

1 tsp pure vanilla powder

1 tsp ground cinnamon

¾ tsp ground cardamom

Tiny pinch of salt

2 small pears (or 1 large), washed, cored and thinly sliced, divided

Ground cinnamon for sprinkling

Coconut Whip (page 183) or Vanilla Custard (page 161), to serve, optional

Preheat the oven to 350°F (180°C). Grease a 9-inch (23-cm) pie pan or round baking dish with a little olive oil.

In a small bowl, combine the chia seeds with water and mix well.

In a large mixing bowl, whisk together the milk, oil and syrup. Add the chia mix and whisk to combine thoroughly. Tip the flour, meal, baking powder, vanilla, cinnamon, cardamom and salt into the bowl and stir to combine well.

Pour half the batter into the prepared pie dish and evenly scatter with half of the pear slices.

Pour the remaining batter over the pears and, if necessary, smooth over the surface with a silicone spatula. Arrange the remaining pear slices on top in a rustic, random fashion or get decorative!

Bake the pudding in the oven for 25 to 30 minutes or until the edges and center have set with a light golden brown crust, but there is still some moisture and perhaps a bit of "wobble" remaining. Do not overbake.

Remove from the oven when done, sprinkle with a little cinnamon and allow the pudding to cool in the pie dish for a few minutes before serving warm with a dollop of Coconut Whip or drizzle of Vanilla Custard, if you like.

 Naturally Sweet Vegan Treats

Blueberry Crumble for Two

Gluten- and grain-free with oil-free and no natural sweetener options | Makes 2 generous servings

Crumble is a comfort dish in its own right and not merely a lazy person's version of pie, though admittedly this one is particularly simple and quick to throw together. This non-traditional version of the crowd-pleasing treat uses frozen blueberries which are extra juicy when they've defrosted and can be enjoyed all year-round. The crumble component skimps on all the things I grew up associating with crumbles—namely flour, butter and sugar, using instead whole foods such as nuts, coconut and spices in conjunction with naturally sweet berries and banana. A perfect dessert to share with someone you love or a quick treat (plus an extra rainy day portion) to enjoy for yourself!

---

1 large ripe banana

1 cup (135 g) frozen blueberries, at least partially thawed for 20 minutes

1 tbsp (15 ml) coconut oil or coconut butter

3 tbsp (18 g) unsweetened desiccated coconut

3 tbsp (28 g) raw almonds, finely chopped

3 tbsp (18 g) hazelnut or almond flour

1 tsp ground cinnamon

¼ tsp pure vanilla powder

¼ tsp ground cardamom

Tiny pinch of stevia, optional

Preheat the oven to 350°F (180°C).

Slice the banana into rounds approximately ⅙ inch (4 mm) thick. Lay the banana slices around the base of 2 ramekins with a capacity of 1½ cups (360 ml) each. Top the banana slices with the partially thawed blueberries.

Combine the oil, coconut, almonds, flour, cinnamon, vanilla, cardamom and stevia (if using) in a medium-size mixing bowl. Top the blueberries in each ramekin with an equal amount of crumble mix, patting it down ever so slightly.

To make a single large crumble, layer the ingredients in an 8-inch (20-cm) pie pan.

Bake the crumble pots on the center rack of the oven for 15 minutes or until the topping is a toasty golden brown, checking on them at the 10-minute mark. If they are browning too quickly, cover the tops loosely with a suitably sized piece of foil for the remainder of the baking time.

Remove the ramekins from the oven and allow the crumble to cool for 10 minutes before serving.

Please note that the pots may still be hot to touch, so mind your fingers while you dig in.

Recipe Notes: To make these crumble pots free from natural added sweetener, omit the stevia.

To save a portion for later, cover it, pop it in the fridge for up to 3 days and reheat it using a microwave for 45 seconds to gently warm through or a preheated oven at 350°F (180°C) for 5 minutes.

Apple Pie Dumplings

Makes 12 dumplings or 4 servings

Love the flavor of apple pie but want to try something new? This recipe's for you! I love savory dumplings, don't get me wrong—I was partly raised on yum cha in Adelaide's Chinatown—but there's something very gratifying about autumnal kitchen experiments born out of a desire to maximize the comfort factor. And these pan-fried balls of dough combined with warm and inviting spiced apple pie filling are a perfect treat for a cozy night in.

Sautéed Apple Pie Filling

1 tbsp (15 ml) coconut oil

2 large tart apples, peeled, cored and cut into ¼-inch (6-mm) pieces

2 tsp (6 g) cornstarch + ¾ cup (180 ml) cold water

2 tbsp (18 g) coconut sugar

1 tsp ground cinnamon

¼ tsp ground allspice

Dumplings

1½ cups (225 g) raisins, soaked in boiled water for 3 minutes

3½ tbsp (52 ml) aquafaba, whisked until lightly foamy and thickened (but not whipped)

1 cup (160 g) + ¼ cup (30 g) organic all-purpose flour, packed and leveled, divided

1½ tsp (7 g) baking powder

Pinch of salt

⅓ cup (30 g) unsweetened desiccated coconut

¼ cup + 2 tsp (70 ml) water + more if needed

1 tbsp (15 ml) coconut oil for frying

Coconut Whip (page 183) or Vanilla Custard (page 161), to serve, optional

To make the apple pie filling, melt the oil over medium heat in a large skillet or saucepan. Add the apples. Cook, stirring constantly, until the apples are almost tender, about 6 to 7 minutes. Dissolve the cornstarch in the water and add the mix to the apples. Stir in the coconut sugar, cinnamon and allspice. Continue to cook for 2 minutes, stirring occasionally. Remove from the heat and set to the side until needed. You can warm the apples up gently over low heat just before serving with the dumplings.

To make the dumplings, start by draining the raisins. Blitz the raisins, aquafaba, flour, baking powder, salt, coconut and water together in a food processor until a dough forms. The dough will be sticky.

Spread the extra ¼ cup (30 g) of flour onto a clean work surface. This will ensure the dough is workable and won't stick. Tip the dough onto the flour. Form into a flour-dusted log, then cut into 12 slices of equal size and roll them into round dumplings.

In a large pan of water over medium-high heat on a gentle boil, simmer 6 dumplings at a time for 4 to 5 minutes. If they stick to the bottom of the pot, give them a little flick to dislodge. As they cook they should begin to float.

Add the coconut oil to a large skillet pan and heat it. Drain the simmered dumplings and pop them into the skillet pan.

Fry the dumplings until they turn golden brown, giving the pan a shake from time to time to ensure even cooking.

Divide the dumplings among bowls, top with spoonfuls of apple pie filling and serve warm.

For added indulgence, top the dumplings with Coconut Whip or Vanilla Custard.

Naturally Sweet Vegan Treats

Persimmon & Almond Baked Pudding

Gluten- and grain-free | Makes 8 servings

Anyone who grew up with a British pudding tradition influencing their culinary experiences will agree that custard and pudding are virtually synonymous. Here you'll find the inviting texture of warm pudding, baked fruit and a light creaminess that subtly evokes baked custard, combined in a single dish. This pudding doesn't require an accompaniment, but I heartily recommend warm Vanilla Custard (page 161) and, for a fun and unique way to serve this, double up on the persimmon. How? In advance of making the pudding itself, simply cut the tops from very ripe (ripeness is crucial) persimmons and freeze them for four to six hours. When you're ready to serve the pudding, simply let the persimmon defrost slightly, spoon out the frozen fruit and pop it on top! Easiest. Nice-cream. Ever.

---

2 tbsp (28 g) chia or flax seeds, finely ground + ½ cup (120 ml) water

1¾ cups (185 g) almond flour

½ cup (60 g) buckwheat flour

¼ cup (35 g) coconut sugar + ½ tsp extra for sprinkling over

1 tsp baking powder

Pinch of salt

½ tsp ground cinnamon

Pinch of ground nutmeg

1½ cups (360 ml) full-fat coconut milk

3 tbsp (45 ml) olive oil

1 tsp pure vanilla extract

2 ripe persimmons, peeled and sliced

2 tbsp (20 g) chopped almonds

Persimmon dairy-free ice cream, maple syrup or Vanilla Custard (page 161), for serving, optional

Preheat the oven to 350°F (180°C). Lightly grease a 10 × 7 inch (26 × 18 cm) baking dish with a little olive oil.

In a small dish, combine the ground chia seeds and water, mixing briskly with a teaspoon. Set the mix to the side.

In a large mixing bowl, combine the almond flour, buckwheat flour, sugar, baking powder, salt, cinnamon and nutmeg.

In a small bowl, whisk the milk, oil, vanilla and chia mix together. Gradually add the liquid mixture to the dry ingredients and mix until no lumps are present.

Pour the batter into the prepared baking dish. Arrange the persimmon slices on top of the batter in a single even layer, leaving a little space between each slice. Scatter the chopped almonds and some coconut sugar over the top. Place the dish on the center rack of the oven and bake the pudding for 35 minutes, or until the middle is set and a toothpick inserted in the center comes out clean.

Allow the pudding to cool slightly, and serve slices/scoops of pudding as is or with persimmon nice-cream and/or a drizzle of maple syrup or Vanilla Custard if desired.

Recipe Note: Any type of commonly available American or Asian persimmon variety should work in this recipe. However, do ensure they are adequately ripe, particularly if using Hachiya, as they can be astringent if not ripe enough. If you can't find persimmons, try this pudding with apricots or plums, bearing in mind that the size of a persimmon is larger than the typical plum or apricot. You will probably require 4 to 6 small stone fruits to replace the quantity of persimmons used in this recipe.

Saffron Semolina Pudding

Low-oil | Makes 6-8 servings

Exotic saffron and warm semolina: the perfect comfort combo? It holds a special place in my heart, in any case! There was a rather grim and gloomy period in my teenage foodie life when the height of my culinary efforts amounted to heating a can of baked beans in a saucepan. Thankfully, when I first moved away from the family home, I found myself living on the same street as a restaurant specializing in vegetarian Indian food. I was near enough broke, their food was incredibly inexpensive for the quality, and they had an all-you-can-eat policy. As such, I found myself there rather often.

To this day, the semolina pudding they served is one of my ultimate comfort desserts, and I've yet to encounter better in any restaurant elsewhere. Here is a version that hits the spot, yet is far lighter on sugar and fat, while also omitting the dairy-based ghee most commonly found in traditional Indian semolina pudding recipes.

Small pinch of saffron +
1 tbsp (15 ml) boiled water, or
powdered saffron without water

2 tbsp (30 ml) coconut oil

1¼ cups (210 g) semolina

2 cups (540 ml) water

1 cup (240 ml) coconut milk + extra
if needed

¼–⅓ cup (35–50 g) coconut sugar
(sweeten to taste)

1–1½ tsp (2–4 g) ground cardamom
(to taste)

1 tsp ground cinnamon

⅓ cup (35 g) chopped toasted
almonds

⅓ cup (60 g) pitted medjool dates,
chopped into small pieces

⅓ cup (50 g) sultanas or raisins

Coconut Whip (page 183), Vanilla
Custard (page 161) or Orange
Cashew Custard (page 136), for
serving, optional

Start by soaking the saffron strands in the boiled water in a small dish or glass. Allow to infuse until the saffron mix is needed.

In a deep pan over low-medium heat, add the coconut oil. Add the semolina and stir to combine it with the oil. Stirring frequently, toast the semolina until it becomes light golden in color and fragrantly toasty in aroma. This should take 7 to 8 minutes. Remove the pan from the heat and set it to the side.

In a separate medium-size saucepan over medium heat, bring the water, milk, sugar, cardamom, cinnamon and saffron liquid mix (or powdered saffron) to a gentle simmer, stirring often.

Place the semolina pan back onto the stove over low-medium heat and carefully ladle the liquid mixture over the semolina mix, stirring briskly to prevent lumps from forming. If any lumps do form, break them apart with your spoon to achieve a smooth paste-like consistency. Add the almonds, dates and sultanas to the pudding mix and stir through.

Cook the mixture until it has thickened and comes away from the sides of the pan easily. At this point you can add extra coconut milk, stirring it in to achieve a slightly less thickened consistency, if preferred.

Turn off the heat and allow the pudding to cool slightly before serving in individual bowls.

Make this pudding extra scrumptious by serving it with a dollop of Coconut Whip, a generous drizzle of coconut milk, Vanilla Custard or Orange Cashew Custard.

 Naturally Sweet Vegan Treats

Blackberry Bread & Butter Pudding

Low added sweetener, nut-free | Makes 6-10 servings

Nothing says comfort treat quite like pudding. Not only is this recipe the perfect way to make good use of bread that's heading to the stale side of the spectrum, but with its own rustic show-stopper charm, it's a perfect brunch or dessert treat to share with friends. With less than ⅓ of a teaspoon of added sweetener per serving, this is a pudding that warmly invites you to help yourself to seconds. An inviting addition to any breakfast, lunch or afternoon tea spread!

---

1 tsp pure vanilla powder

1¾ cups (420 ml) unsweetened coconut or cashew milk

1¾ cups (380 g) silken tofu

1½ tsp (4 g) arrowroot powder, optional

Pinch of ground nutmeg

¼ tsp ground cardamom

1 tbsp (9 g) coconut sugar

⅓ cup (65 g) well stirred coconut butter or ⅓ cup (80 ml) light olive oil + a little extra for greasing

10–12 thick slices bread

Approximately 2 tsp (5 g) ground cinnamon

¾–1 cup (130–175 g) pitted medjool dates, finely chopped

1½ cups (190 g) frozen or fresh blackberries

Coconut Whip (page 183), for serving, optional

Preheat the oven to 340°F (170°C) convection or 350°F (180°C) non-convection. Use a small amount of coconut butter or oil to grease a 15-cup (3.6-L) ovenproof dish roughly 12½ × 7 inches (32 × 18 cm) with a depth of 3 inches (8 cm).

To make the custard, simply blitz the vanilla, milk, tofu, arrowroot, nutmeg, cardamom and sugar in a blender or food processor until smooth and creamy. Set the custard to the side while you assemble your pudding.

Spread a little of the coconut butter (alternatively, brush olive oil) over both sides of each slice of bread before sprinkling them lightly with cinnamon. Cut the bread slices into squares (like large croutons) or halve them diagonally, then place half of the pieces, slightly overlapping, into the dish.

Drop two-thirds of the date pieces evenly over the bread. Scatter two-thirds of the blackberries over the bread. Top the first layer of bread with a second layer of bread. Pour the custard over the bread. Top the pudding with an even scattering of the remaining date pieces and blackberries.

Leave the pudding to sit for 15 minutes to allow the bread to soak up the custard, then place the dish into the oven and bake for 35 to 40 minutes, or until golden and toasty.

Once baked, allow the pudding to cool slightly before serving along with a light drizzle of maple syrup or lashings of Coconut Whip (page 183), if you wish!

Recipe Note: Coconut butter is essentially the oil and flesh from fresh coconut, whipped into a spread. If you'd prefer to use vegan buttery spread or margarine, it works too.

Raw & Unbaked

No-bake treats and desserts

Neapolitan Ice-Cream Cake

Gluten-free | Makes about 18 servings

Looking for homemade dairy- and egg-free ice cream alternatives that don't involve bananas or an ice-cream maker? You are in luck! For those who feel a pang of nostalgia when you hear the words "Neapolitan ice cream," you're also in luck! This ice-cream cake combines the classic Neapolitan flavor trio of chocolate, strawberry and vanilla along with all-natural flavors, plant-based creaminess and contemporary visual appeal. And it's surprisingly easy to put together. Of course, it is much lower in sugar than the freezer staple of many a suburban home of the 1980s too. Great to prep and make in advance of a celebration, it's a pretty party treat.

Ice-Cream Cake

2½ cups (360 g) cashews, soaked overnight in a large bowl (or 2 hours with boiling water poured over)

1⅓ cups (315 ml) full-fat coconut milk

⅓ cup (80 ml) maple syrup (or more to taste)

1 tbsp (15 ml) vanilla extract

¼ cup + 1 tbsp (38 g) raw cacao powder

¼ cup (40 g) chopped dark chocolate, optional (but recommended)

¾ cup (166 g) frozen strawberries, defrosted

8 freeze-dried strawberries

½ tsp lemon juice

Chocolate Drizzle

¼ cup (40 g) chopped chocolate

½ tbsp (22 ml) coconut oil

Line a loaf pan with parchment paper—the neater the lining, the "cleaner" the end result will be. Set it aside.

Drain the cashews, then add them, the milk, syrup and vanilla to a high-powered blender (or food processor) and blitz until the mix is creamy and as smooth as possible. Taste the mix to check the level of sweetness. Add more syrup if desired and blend again.

Pour ¾ cup (180 ml) of this mix into a separate bowl and set it to the side. Divide the remaining mix equally between two additional bowls. Pour the contents from one of these last two bowls back into the blender, add the cacao powder and blitz to incorporate well. Add the chopped chocolate (if using) and give it a quick blitz. The chocolate doesn't have to be completely blended in, as a speckled effect is quite nice. Once blended to your liking, pour this chocolate layer mix carefully into the prepared pan. Smooth the surface over with a silicone spatula if needed. Pop the pan in the freezer for 15 minutes.

Rinse out the blender and tip into it the reserved ¾ cup (180 ml) of mix. Add the defrosted frozen strawberries, freeze-dried strawberries and lemon juice. Blitz this mix to create the strawberry ice-cream layer mix. Set this to the side for the time being.

After 15 minutes in the freezer, carefully remove the pan with the chocolate layer.

Take the bowl containing plain mix in it and carefully pour it over the chocolate layer. Smooth the surface using a silicone spatula if necessary. Pop the pan back in the freezer for a further 15 minutes.

(continued)

Neapolitan Ice-Cream Cake (Continued)

Remove the pan from the freezer and carefully pour in the strawberry mix. Again, use a silicone spatula to create a smooth surface. Cover the pan with foil to prevent freezer burn and place it back in the freezer, allowing the ice-cream cake to completely freeze through, about 6 hours.

When ready to serve, turn out the cake and remove the parchment paper. Allow the cake to thaw slightly for about 15 to 20 minutes for ease of cutting. Prepare the chocolate drizzle by gently melting ¼ cup (40 g) of chopped chocolate together with the coconut oil.

Drizzle the ice-cream cake with the melted chocolate, slice it with a sharp knife and serve the slices immediately.

Recipe Notes: Defrosted frozen strawberries are incredibly juicy, yet the freeze-dried ones add both flavor and color enhancement without the extra water content, so a mix of both works well.

You can use an 8 × 8 inch (20 × 20 cm) brownie pan with an 8-cup (1.9-L) capacity to make a square slab cake, if you prefer.

Rocky Road with Berry Gummies
Gluten-free | Makes 12-20 pieces

This two-part recipe is my rather more adult-friendly and satiating—a little goes a long way—take on the tooth-achingly-sweet rocky road of my childhood. There used to be a very famous sweet shop on a busy street corner in the heart of Adelaide. Growing up, I'd venture in around December when we made the annual family trek to visit Father Christmas at the nearby department store. And the rocky road on display, wrapped in clear plastic to show off the contents inside is, for some reason, one of my most vivid childhood Christmas memories. Packed to the brim with peanuts, coconut and plump marshmallows, it was a sight to behold. Each year I was like a kid in a candy store. Literally and figuratively. My modern-day rocky road sees gelatin-based marshmallows replaced with vegan-friendly, semi-sweet agar-agar berry gummies, which have their own alluring appeal. Boasting mixed nuts, coconut and homemade gummies encased in dark chocolate, this rocky road is a festively semi-sweet chocolate indulgence.

Red Berry Gummies —thick jell

1½ cups (200 g) frozen mixed red berries (strawberries, lingonberries, raspberries and red currants all work well, but try to mix sweet with tart)

½ cup (120 ml) water

1 tsp maple syrup, optional

2 tbsp (4 g) agar-agar flakes
2 tsp (3g) powder

Rocky Road

1⅓ cups (235 g) chopped dark chocolate

1 tbsp (15 ml) coconut oil

1 tsp maple syrup, optional

½ cup (70 g) almonds (raw or toasted)

½ cup (70 g) cashew or macadamia nuts (raw or toasted)

¼ cup (35 g) unsweetened desiccated coconut

2 tsp (5 g) coconut flour, for dusting

To make the gummies, line a loaf pan with parchment paper or have a silicone mold with small shapes ready to go. In a medium-size saucepan, gently warm the frozen berries, water and syrup (if using) over low-medium heat, allowing the berries to soften and defrost. Stir occasionally. This should take about 5 minutes.

Remove the pan from the heat and use either an immersion blender placed directly in the pot to blend the berries to a fine purée or tip the mix into a blender to give it a good whizz. Add the agar-agar flakes to the saucepan along with the puréed berries and mix well.

Set the saucepan with the berry and agar-agar mix back onto the stove and, over medium heat, bring the mixture to a bubbling simmer. Whisking constantly, allow the mix to continue to simmer for 2 minutes. Remove the pan from the heat and pour the mix into the loaf pan or silicone mold.

Place the gummies in the fridge for at least 2 to 3 hours to set. If making cut gummies, remove the gummy slab carefully from the tray and cut it into squares approximately ⅜ inch (10 mm) in size.

To assemble the rocky road, gently melt the chocolate in a double boiler over low heat. Add the oil and syrup (if using), stirring to combine well. Remove the bowl from the heat and allow the melted mixture to cool for 5 to 10 minutes, making sure it remains in a pourable form.

(continued)

Rocky Road with Berry Gummies (Continued)

Line a loaf pan with parchment paper. In a large mixing bowl, combine the nuts, about three-fourths of the gummies and the coconut. Pour in the chocolate mix and fold gently using a silicone spatula or spoon, so that all the goodies are coated but the gummies don't break apart.

Tip the rocky road mix into the loaf pan and press it down gently with the spatula or spoon. Place the pan in the fridge for at least 2 hours to set.

To serve, turn out the slab and cut it into slices/chunks of a roughly even size, then dust with a little coconut flour.

Recipe Notes: If you want to get a little fancy, consider sprinkling Unicorn Sprinkles (page 201) or edible dried flower petals over your rocky road in place of, or in conjunction with, the dusting of coconut flour.

Eat the remaining gummies as snacks or store them in the fridge for up to 5 days in an airtight container (or in the freezer for up to 3 months).

No time to make the gummies? Use dried fruit (such as dried blueberries, cranberries or chopped apricots) or all-natural vegan marshmallows instead.

If agar-agar flakes cannot be found, 2 teaspoons (3 g) of agar-agar powder can be used in their place, but please be careful not to confuse the amounts or you will end up with little gummy bricks.

Peanut Butter Crisp Bites

Gluten-free | Makes 16-20 pieces

Peanut butter lovers, raise your hands! We cannot get enough peanut butter in our home and are seemingly on a lifelong quest to find new ways to enjoy it. It often makes an appearance at breakfast, and it's my husband's go-to snack option to spread on sourdough when the baked treat stashes run low. These little snacks are no less tasty than classic peanut butter on toast, but perhaps a tad more exciting. A marriage of peanut butter–flavored soft fudginess and crispy crackle, these bites make perfect party treats, mid-afternoon snacks or cheeky Netflix-watching nibbles.

½ cup (125 g) unsweetened peanut butter

3½ tbsp (50 ml) coconut oil

3½ tbsp (50 ml) coconut milk

3 tbsp (45 ml) maple syrup

1 tsp vanilla extract

Pinch of salt

½ cup (15 g) crispy puffed rice cereal + ⅓ cup (10 g) extra for sprinkling

½ cup (60 g) unsweetened desiccated coconut

Line a brownie pan with parchment paper. In a medium-size saucepan, combine the peanut butter, oil, milk, syrup, vanilla and salt over low heat and mix well with a spoon to incorporate.

Fold in the crispy rice cereal and coconut. Pour the mix into the lined pan and smooth over the surface with a silicone spatula or the back of a large metal spoon. Sprinkle the extra rice cereal evenly over the surface of the mix, then press down gently using a silicone spatula or the back of a large metal spoon.

Refrigerate the slab for at least an hour. When set, remove the pan from the fridge and wait a few minutes before slicing the slab into squares with a sharp knife.

For maximum crackle factor, eat the bites as close to slicing as possible. It is possible to store uneaten pieces in the refrigerator and serve them cold (direct from the fridge), but they won't be as crunchy on top.

Recipe Notes: Crispy rice cereal may contain traces of gluten, so if you are sensitive, please opt for a certified gluten-free variety.

Conventional crispy rice cereal contains added sugar, so look for a sugar-free brand if that is an issue for you. Even if using a conventional brand, the small amount of cereal required for this recipe means that any added sugar contributed to the mix would amount to ½ teaspoon for the entire batch, which is negligible.

Mocha Balls

No added unrefined sweetener, nut-free with gluten-free option |
Makes 6 large balls or 12 mini balls

One of Sweden's favorite treats, reimagined. Chokladbollar are sweet and chocolaty, understandably popular, mildly mocha flavored—which I personally love—oat-based balls. They are kind of like sugar-laden bliss balls, but have been around long before bliss balls were a thing and obviously never associated with healthy eating. They can be fashioned from margarine and organic white sugar to make them technically vegan and, in fact, Sweden's most popular commercially produced brand of chokladboll is believed to be accidentally vegan. Having said that, traditional Chokladboll versions—both store-bought and homemade—can contain more refined sugar and processed fat than they do oats, gram for gram. Needless to say, they are probably not the healthiest snack option this country has to offer. There is a solution, though, for those of us who generally prefer a slightly more wholesome treat. Make them from scratch, of course!

¾ cup + 1 tbsp (80 g) organic rolled oats

½ cup (44 g) unsweetened desiccated coconut, divided

11–12 pitted medjool dates

2 tbsp (15 g) raw cacao powder

2 tbsp (30 ml) coconut oil, melted

½ tsp pure vanilla powder

Pinch of salt

¼ cup (60 ml) cooled coffee (decaf, if preferred) + extra if required

Blitz the oats, ¼ cup (22 g) of the coconut, dates, cacao, oil, vanilla, salt and coffee in a food processor to form a workable dough. Add extra coffee if the mix seems too dry to bring together.

Spread the remaining coconut onto a large dinner plate. Using your hands, form the mix into individual balls of equal size and roll them in the coconut.

For a unicorn version, drizzle the balls with melted dairy-free white chocolate and decorate with Unicorn Sprinkles (page 201).

The Mocha Balls can be stored in an airtight container in the fridge for up to a week or frozen for up to 3 months.

Recipe Note: To make the balls entirely gluten-free, use gluten-free oats.

Naturally Sweet Vegan Treats

No-Bake Love Yummies (Kärleksmums) ✓+

Gluten- and grain-free | Makes 16-20 pieces

"What are love yummies?" you may well ask. To begin with, *love yummy* is the rather cute literal translation of kärleksmums, the name of a chocolaty baked brownie-reminiscent treat widely available and beloved across Sweden. I have never seen them made here without coconut sprinkled on top, but as this no-bake, vegan version is not a traditional recipe by any stretch of the imagination, I won't hold it against you if you decide to use grated chocolate, cacao nibs or nothing at all on yours! Share something yummy with those you love!

---

1 cup (140 g) almonds

1½ cups (225 g) cashews

12 pitted medjool dates soaked in ⅓ cup + 2 tsp (90 ml) freshly boiled water

3 tbsp (45 ml) coconut oil

2 tbsp (30 ml) maple syrup

⅓ cup (35 g) raw cacao powder

Pinch of pure vanilla powder

Pinch of salt

Frosting

1 cup (240 ml) full-fat, organic canned coconut milk (use as much of the cream as possible)

⅓ cup + 1 tbsp (45 g) raw cacao powder

3 tbsp (40 g) chia seeds, finely ground

2–2½ tbsp (30–38 ml) maple syrup

Unsweetened desiccated coconut, for sprinkling

Blitz the almonds and cashews to a crumb texture in a food processor or blender.

Add the dates and the water they've been soaking in, oil, syrup, cacao, vanilla and salt, and continue to pulse until you have a sticky yet workable dough. Press the mix into a rectangular 11 × 17 inch (18 × 28 cm) baking dish or brownie pan.

Prepare the frosting by combining the creamy coconut milk, cacao powder, chia seeds and syrup in a bowl and whisking until smooth.

The frosting mix should start to thicken almost immediately, but continue to whisk for another minute. Using a silicone spatula or the back of a large metal spoon, spread the frosting evenly over the raw cake slab.

Sprinkle desiccated coconut over the frosting. Set the cake in the fridge for 4 hours or overnight.

Slice into squares before serving. These treats are sweet (think along the lines of a raw bliss ball), so a little piece goes a long way.

Recipe Note: If you want to dress them up for a special occasion, consider sprinkling them with Unicorn Sprinkles (page 201) or edible dried flower petals.

Raw Gingerbread Cookies

Gluten- and grain-free with fructose-free option | Makes 20 small cookies

Advent is the time of year when Sweden takes its fika culture to another level. Offices, homes, schools and cafés around the country are filled with baskets of buns and trays of cookies, most notably the ubiquitous Swedish gingerbread cookie. Indeed pepparkakor, as they are known, are the must-have treat at every Swedish Advent fika gathering. Unlike the ultra sweet and crisp cookies that Sweden has made famous, this recipe produces raw cookies that are rather fudgy in texture and lightly sweetened. Great make-ahead treats, simply remove them from the fridge or freezer when you or your guests want a quick, healthier and rather more satiating festive snack. Say hello to Sweden's favorite cookie, reimagined!

½ cup (70 g) almonds

¼ cup (30 g) pecans

½ cup + 2 tbsp (95 g) cashews

1¼ tsp (3 g) ground ginger

1¾ tsp (4 g) ground cinnamon

¼ tsp ground cardamom

¾ tsp ground cloves

1½ tbsp (23 ml) coconut oil, melted

2½ tbsp (38 ml) maple syrup

1–2 tbsp (7–14 g) coconut flour, for dusting, optional

Process the almonds, pecans and cashews to a coarse flour texture in a food processor. Add the ginger, cinnamon, cardamom, cloves, oil and syrup and blitz until a sticky dough forms. Taste-test the dough. Want more spice? Add a pinch or two extra of all the spices.

Roll out the dough to a thickness of ⅛ inch (4 mm) between two sheets of parchment paper lightly dusted with coconut or almond flour.

Using small cookie cutters, cut out shapes. The off-cuts can be balled back together and re-rolled to make more cookies.

Using a small sieve, dust lightly with coconut flour before serving, if you like.

Store the cookies in the fridge for up to 5 days, covered. Or store in the freezer up to 3 months, separated by layers of cut parchment paper in an airtight container.

Recipe Note: To make the cookies fructose-free, use rice malt syrup instead of maple syrup.

Naturally Sweet Vegan Treats

Strawberries & Cream Fudge

Low-fructose, gluten- and nut-free options | Makes 16-20 pieces

Not everyone adores chocolate—shocking, I know—and my daughter will certainly always pick something fruit flavored over any other type of sweet treat if given a choice. So if you (or someone you'd like to spoil) have a sweet tooth and a soft spot for all things fruity, these delicately flavored, naturally colored fruity freezer fudge bites might be the answer.

I don't typically use any coloring agents in everyday food, but if you come across pitaya or beet powder, they are great alternatives to artificial food coloring, and both impart a natural sweetness to the foods to which they're added. A little goes a long way too, but you can add more to the mix if you prefer a deeper color.

1¾ cups (155 g) rolled oats

½ cup (70 g) frozen strawberries (approximately 10), defrosted

½ cup (120 ml) unsalted, smooth cashew butter

3 tbsp + 1 tsp (50 ml) maple syrup

3 tbsp + 1 tsp (50 ml) coconut oil

1 tbsp (15 ml) nut/oat milk, if needed

2 tsp (10 ml) vanilla extract

¼ tsp stevia powder, optional

1 tbsp (5 g) strawberry powder (from 6 crushed freeze-dried strawberries)

1½ tsp (3 g) pitaya powder or 1 tsp (2 g) beet powder + extra to sprinkle over, optional

Line a small dish or baking pan with parchment paper.

Blitz the oats in a food processor until they reach a coarse flour consistency. Set to the side.

Purée the defrosted strawberries, or mash them well with a fork in a small bowl. Gently warm the puréed strawberries, butter, syrup, oil, milk and vanilla in a medium pan over low heat to bring them together before adding the ground oats and stevia (if using). Stir well to combine.

Alternatively, if you want a smoother fudge batter, or to keep your fudge technically raw, use a food processor to combine the pulsed oats, wet ingredients and stevia (if using).

For a simple, uniformly colored fudge, add the strawberry powder and pitaya or beet powder and pour the mix into the lined dish, smoothing over the surface with a spatula or the back of a large spoon, before placing the fudge into the freezer to set for 30 minutes.

For a slightly fancier two-layer fudge, divide the mixture in half before adding the strawberry powder and pitaya or beet powder. Leave one half as is. To the second half, add the freeze dried strawberry powder and the pitaya or beet powder (if using) and mix well to combine. Place the second portion of fudge mixture with powder added into the lined dish and use a spatula or the back of a large spoon to flatten it out, creating a smooth surface and uniform thickness. Pop the dish in the freezer for 5 minutes. Remove the dish and add the rest of the fudge mix, and continue smoothing out the surface.

(continued)

Strawberries & Cream Fudge (Continued)

Place the fudge in the freezer for 30 minutes to set. Remove the set fudge from the tray and slice it into squares or cut it into shapes using cookie cutters.

Sprinkle the fudge pieces with a light dusting of berry powder and/or edible flowers, if you like. Store this fudge in an airtight container in the freezer for up to 3 months and remove a few minutes before serving. It should be served cold and while fairly firm.

Recipe Notes: For a gluten-free option, use gluten-free oats.

Blonde, unsalted tahini or sunflower seed butter can be used in the case of nut allergy issues.

Replace maple syrup with rice malt syrup for a low-fructose option.

Chocolate Cream Pie "Cheese" Cake

Oil-, gluten- and grain-free | Makes 1 (9-inch [23-cm]) cake
and ²/₃ cup (160 ml) ganache

Pure, unadulterated, whole-food indulgence! I deliberated over whether to include my Raw Rainbow Cake recipe in this book or a recipe decidedly simpler to assemble. Simplicity won. But not at the expense of taste; I hope you'll agree. Creamy, rich and decadent, a little of this cake goes a long way! This chocolaty, fruit-sweetened treat is dedicated to my little brother, who loves to remind me of the time I accidentally destroyed our mum's chocolate cream pie, which was her contribution to a church dinner event. Evidently, I was so fascinated by my own reflection in a mirror as I proudly held the cake that I failed to notice it was slowly sliding off the plate. I truly hope you enjoy this simple and delicious take on raw cake and that you don't repeat my cake-dropping folly!

Crust

1 cup (175 g) pitted dates

½ cup (75 g) dried sultanas or raisins

¾ cup (105 g) almonds

¾ cup (115 g) cashews

3 tbsp (21 g) hazelnut meal

Filling

4 cups (600 g) cashews, soaked in water for at least 4 hours

2 cups (350 g) pitted dates

1½ cups (360 ml) water

1 cup (240 ml) almond or cashew milk

1½ tsp (7 ml) vanilla extract or 1 tsp pure vanilla powder, optional

¾ cup + 1 tbsp (85 g) unsweetened cocoa powder or raw cacao powder

Process the dates, sultanas, almonds, cashews and hazelnut meal in a food processor or high-powered blender until the mixture comes together to form a slightly sticky dough when squashed. Press the dough into a 9-inch (23-cm) spring-form pan to form the crust.

For the filling, blitz the cashews, dates, water, milk and vanilla in a blender until smooth. Remove ¾ to 1 cup (180 to 240 ml) of the mixture and set it aside, covered, in the fridge. Add the cocoa to the remaining mix still in the blender and blend until incorporated. Pour the chocolate mix over the crust and place the cake in the freezer for 2 hours.

After 2 hours, remove the pan from the freezer and spread the remaining mix that was set aside over the top of the cake using a silicone spatula. Place the cake back in the freezer for at least a couple of hours more.

Remove the cake from the freezer 30 minutes before slicing.

(continued)

From-Scratch Basic Chocolate Ganache

⅓ cup + 4 tsp (100 ml) maple/rice malt syrup (or more or less to taste)

3 tbsp (45 ml) coconut oil, melted

⅓ cup (35 g) cacao + more to achieve desired consistency, if needed

Extra toppings and decorations

Fresh berries

Mocha balls (page 116)

Maple-Glazed Dehydrated Citrus Slices (page 200)

If decorating with From-Scratch Basic Chocolate Ganache, add all the syrup, oil and cacao to a small saucepan over low heat, stirring until smooth and well combined.

Remove the pan from the heat and allow the ganache to cool to a point where it is still pourable but not hot. Drizzle it around the top edge of the cake. Top with the extra toppings, if you'd like.

Uneaten portions of cake should be stored in the freezer if there's any left!

Raw Peanut Butter & Choc-Chip Mini Doughnuts

Nut- and gluten-free options | Makes 18 mini doughnuts

The perfect peanut butter–lover's power snack—and oh so cute, too! I first started making simple raw treats on occasion when Lillian was a baby, not so much because I considered going raw at the time, but rather because basic raw goodies are so easy to prep and store and excellent fuel for nursing mamas! They really are a convenient and wholesome grab-and-go treat. And by using silicone molds such as the mini doughnut one used to make these, you can take their kid appeal up a notch too.

1 cup (100 g) gluten-free rolled oats

6 tbsp (37 g) almond meal

3 tbsp (18 g) unsweetened desiccated coconut

2–3 tbsp (15–23 g) raw cacao nibs

¼ tsp ground cinnamon

½ cup + 1 tsp (125 ml) smooth, unsweetened peanut butter

1 tbsp (15 ml) maple syrup

1 tsp vanilla extract

1–3 tbsp (15–45 ml) almond milk + extra if required

Basic Raw Chocolate (page 197), for serving, optional

Pulse the oats in a food processor to a coarse flour consistency. In a large bowl, combine the oats, almond meal, coconut, cacao nibs and cinnamon.

Combine the peanut butter, syrup, vanilla and almond milk in a medium mixing bowl.

Pour the wet ingredients into the dry ingredients and stir everything until well combined, using your hands if you need to. The mixture may seem a little dry at first, but should ultimately stick together. If it doesn't come together, add extra almond milk, a little at a time, until it does.

Press the mix into the holes of a mini silicone doughnut tray, or roll between your palms to form cookie dough balls.

Top with melted Basic Raw Chocolate, if you like.

Freeze or refrigerate to set, 30 minutes to 1 hour, and store unused mini doughnuts/cookie dough balls in an airtight container in your fridge for up to 5 days or in your freezer for up to 3 months.

Recipe Note: To make these nut-free, use sunflower butter in place of peanut butter, use oat milk in place of almond milk and add ¼ cup (25 g) of oats in place of the almond meal.

Choc-Hazelnut Truffle Bites

Gluten- and grain-free with low-fructose and nut-free options | Makes 16-32 truffle bites

Rich, chocolaty and satisfying bite-size treats. As a long-time lover of a certain chocolaty, hazelnutty spread, I can safely say these truffles hit the spot. Based on one of my most popular blog recipes to date, I truly think this particular version takes things to the next level. Our baby Oliver has been known to use these to create a chocolate face mask of sorts. I don't recommend trying this. They are, however, the perfect make-ahead treats. Simply prep and decorate them in advance and, as required, these delicious bites can be served direct from the freezer. Easy!

¾ cup (130 g) 85–90% cocoa chopped chocolate

2 tbsp (30 ml) coconut oil

¾ cup (180 g) hazelnut butter

½ tbsp (7 ml) maple syrup

3½ tbsp (26 g) raw cacao

Pinch of salt

Pinch of pure vanilla powder

¼ cup (45 g) chopped hazelnuts, optional

Cacao powder, coconut or dried flower sprinkles of choice, to decorate

Line an 8 × 8 inch (20 × 20 cm) square baking pan with parchment paper. A smaller sized pan can be used, if preferred, but not larger.

In a double boiler over low heat, combine the chocolate and the coconut oil. Melt together, stirring to incorporate towards the end of the melting time.

When melted and smooth, add the hazelnut butter and mix thoroughly. Add the syrup, cacao, salt and vanilla. Mix well.

Remove from the heat and pour the truffle mix into the prepared pan and smooth the surface using a silicone spatula.

Pop the pan in the freezer for 1 hour or until the mix is firm and set.

Carefully lift the truffle slab out of the tray and place it on a cutting board. Cut the slab into 16 squares or 32 triangles by slicing each square on the diagonal.

Decorate your truffles with chopped nuts and sprinkles if desired.

Store your truffles in the freezer and remember to serve them very cold, as they don't fare well for long at room temperature.

Recipe Notes: Tahini can replace the hazelnut butter for a nut-free option, but of course, the flavor profile will be very different.

If you are mindful of fructose, replace the maple syrup with organic rice malt syrup.

Naturally Sweet Vegan Treats

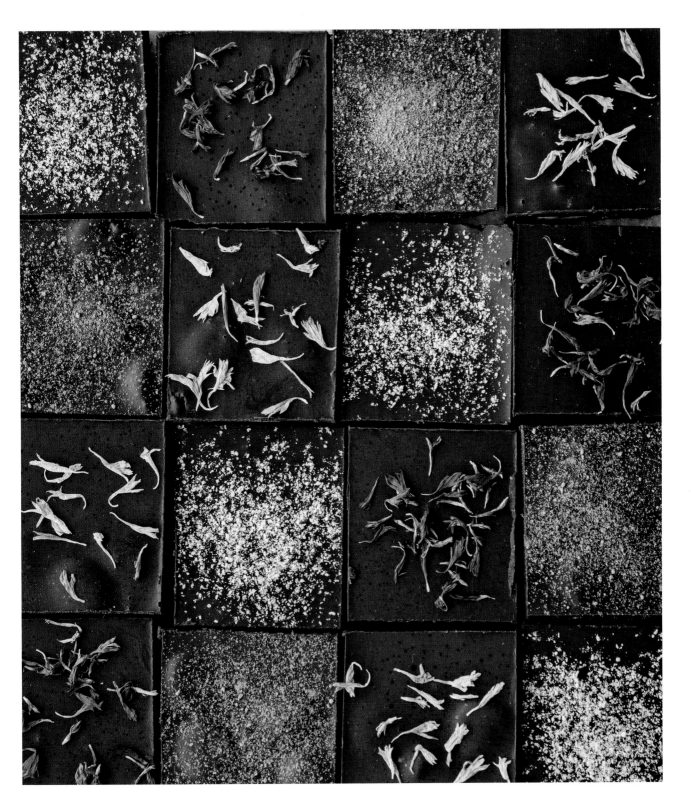

Celebaking

Cakes, treats and seasonal goodies,
perfect for celebrations

Banana Kladdkaka

With just 1 teaspoon of added sweetener per serving, this version of Kladdkaka, which translates literally from Swedish to English as gooey or messy cake, is anything but traditional! A staple sweet treat found in cafés, homes and party venues across Sweden, the traditional version of this dense and sticky chocolate cake has a brownie-like exterior and a soft, gooey center—and a single serving easily contains a whopping 10 to 12 teaspoons (40-48 g) of white sugar before adding the sweetened cream or ice-cream! This lighter version has a banana-y twist and contains just 1 teaspoon of maple syrup per serving. Eat it warm just as it is, or try a slice with a dollop of Coconut Whip (page 183) and some fresh or frozen berries.

---

2 tbsp (28 g) chia seeds, finely ground + ⅓ cup + 2 tbsp (110 ml) water

2½ tbsp (38 ml) coconut oil, melted + extra for greasing the pan

Buckwheat flour, for dusting cake pan

⅓ cup (80 g) mashed ripe banana

1 cup + 1 tbsp (70 g) almond flour

⅓ cup + 1 tbsp (95 ml) unsweetened cashew or almond milk, at room temperature

3 tbsp (45 ml) maple syrup

¼ cup (25 g) cacao powder or pure unsweetened cocoa powder

1 tsp pure vanilla powder

Coconut flour, berries and Coconut Whip (page 183), for serving

Recipe Note: To reduce the fructose content in the cake, replace the banana with ⅓ cup (80 g) of cooked, mashed sweet potato and substitute rice malt syrup for maple syrup.

Mix the chia seeds with the water, stirring quickly to incorporate well. The mix should jell almost immediately, but set it to the side.

Preheat the oven to 350°F (180 °C). Grease an 8-inch (20-cm) springform pan with melted coconut oil and dust it lightly with buckwheat flour.

Mix the chia mix, oil, banana, flour, milk, syrup, cacao and vanilla in a food processor or blender until all the ingredients are incorporated and a smooth batter has formed. Fill the prepared pan with cake batter, smoothing the surface out with a silicone spatula.

Bake the cake in the center of the oven for 20 to 25 minutes. When ready, the cake's center should be set but not overly firm, so do keep an eye on it as the baking time comes to an end.

Because all ovens are calibrated a little differently, your bake time may vary slightly. Twenty-three minutes in my oven results in a set cake with a very gooey (but not molten) center, but if you remove your cake earlier or if it needs a minute or so longer, don't worry; it will still be delicious regardless of set. This cake is traditionally very flat and even the old-school versions containing eggs are not designed to rise. And remember that this cake is meant to be a little messy, but because it's completely plant-based, even the gooiest of centers is safe to eat.

Remove the cake from the oven and set it on a coaster to cool slightly for 5 minutes, then run a knife along the inside edge of the pan to loosen the side of the cake if necessary. Carefully release the springform mechanism on the pan. Allow the cake to cool for at least 15 minutes more before serving. If the cake is particularly gooey in texture, allowing it to cool at room temperature longer or set in the refrigerator will aid slicing.

Decorate the cake with a light dusting of coconut flour and serve it with berries and Coconut Whip.

Orange Loaf Cake

Nut-free | Makes 1 loaf and 1¹/₂ cups (360 ml) custard

Perfect for sharing with a crowd, this orange cake is moist and delicious and a great alternative to banana bread for those looking for something a little different. It is delightful as is, but can be further spruced up with the addition of a drizzle of the Orange Cashew Custard.

Orange Loaf Cake

2 cups (260 g) all-purpose flour

1 tbsp (9 g) cornstarch

2 tsp (9 g) baking powder

½ tsp baking soda

Pinch of salt

⅓ cup (50 g) coconut sugar

Zest of 2 naval oranges, finely grated

⅓ cup + 2 tsp (100 ml) coconut oil, melted + extra for greasing the pan

⅓ cup (80 ml) maple syrup

¼ cup + 1 tbsp (75 ml) oat or soy yogurt

¼ cup (60 ml) freshly squeezed orange juice

1½ tsp (7 ml) apple cider vinegar

Orange Cashew Custard

1 (14-oz [400-ml]) can organic coconut milk, chilled well

½ cup (75 g) raw cashews, soaked 4 to 8 hours, drained and rinsed

1½ tbsp (22 ml) coconut oil, melted

1 tbsp (15 ml) maple syrup

1 tbsp (15 ml) water

3 tbsp (45 ml) orange juice

½ tsp vanilla extract

Zest of ½ orange, finely grated

Maple-Glazed Dehydrated Citrus Slices (page 200), for serving

Preheat the oven to 350°F (180°C). Grease a loaf pan and line with parchment paper.

Sift the flour, cornstarch, baking powder, baking soda and salt together into a large mixing bowl. In a medium-size mixing bowl, combine the sugar, zest, oil, syrup, yogurt, juice and vinegar. Pour the wet mix over the dry mix and gently fold through until the wet and dry ingredients have incorporated. Do not overmix.

Pour the cake batter into the lined loaf pan and bake the cake for 30 to 35 minutes or until a skewer inserted in the center comes out clean. Leave the cake to cool in the pan for 15 minutes, then carefully transfer it to a wire rack to cool completely.

To make the custard, blitz the milk, cashews, oil, syrup, water, juice and vanilla until creamy and smooth in a high-powered blender or food processor. Stir in the zest or sprinkle the zest over once the custard is poured. Unless serving the entire cake in one go, I recommend slicing portions and serving them with the custard individually. Top with Maple-Glazed Dehydrated Citrus Slices.

Naturally Sweet Vegan Treats

Go-To Chocolate Cupcakes with Fudge Frosting

Gluten- and grain-free | Makes 14-16 cupcakes

As the name suggests, these are our go-to chocolaty treats in cupcake form. They're a wholesome take on a classic cupcake that are easy-to-bake and fun to dress up as is appropriate for whatever occasion you happen to be celebrating. Moist, delicious and sure to please tea-time or party guests of all ages, they feature far less sugar and oil than their more traditional counterparts and can be made entirely free of gluten too!

Cupcakes

1 tbsp (14 g) chia seeds, finely ground + 5 tbsp water

¾ cup (90 g) buckwheat flour

¼ cup + 3 tbsp (42 g) almond or oat flour

½ cup (60 g) pure unsweetened cocoa powder

3½ tbsp (28 g) arrowroot powder

¼ cup (35 g) + 1 tbsp (15 g) coconut sugar

1 tbsp (14 g) baking powder

Pinch of salt

¼ cup (60 ml) aquafaba

¼ cup (60 ml) olive oil

1 tsp apple cider vinegar

1 tsp vanilla extract

1½ cups (360 ml) oat or almond milk

Fudge Frosting

1 cup (150 g) cashews, soaked for at least 4 hours/overnight and drained

1 cup (175 g) pitted medjool dates

¼ cup + 1 tbsp (38 g) raw cacao powder (or pure unsweetened cocoa powder)

½ tsp pure vanilla powder

Tiny pinch of salt

2 tbsp (30 ml) coconut oil

¼ cup + 1 tbsp (75 ml) water + a tbsp (15 ml) or extra if needed

In a small bowl, mix the chia seeds with the water. Stir quickly and thoroughly with a small spoon. The mix should jell almost immediately, but let it sit for a few minutes while you prepare the rest of the batter.

Sift the flours, cocoa, arrowroot, sugar, baking powder and salt into a large bowl.

In a medium-size mixing bowl, whisk the aquafaba until it is slightly foamy, then continue whisking while adding the oil, vinegar and vanilla. Tip in the chia mix and whisk it through the wet mix to incorporate.

Pour the milk over the dry mix and stir to begin to bring the batter together, then tip in the oil and aquafaba mix and stir until the batter is well combined and smooth. Let the batter rest for 30 minutes. This is where the magic happens. The arrowroot powder needs time to hydrate and thus a little patience is required. If you've ever had issues with arrowroot powder being a little gritty in baked goods, this is the trick to solve that problem!

Meanwhile, preheat the oven to 350°F (180°C) and fill a cupcake tray with cupcake papers.

Prepare the frosting by blitzing the cashews, dates, cacao, vanilla, salt, oil and water in a high-powered blender or food processor until smooth, thick and creamy.

Fill each cupcake liner with 3½ tablespoons (50 ml) of cake batter. Pop the tray on the center rack of the oven and bake the cupcakes for 15 to 16 minutes or until a toothpick inserted in the center of a cupcake comes out clean. Allow the cupcakes to cool completely on a wire rack before frosting.

Frost your cooled cupcakes either by spreading frosting over them or by piping (yes, this frosting is pipeable!) and serve immediately. Unfrosted cupcakes can be frozen and defrosted as you require them.

Chocolate Celebration Cake

Oil-free, nut-free if using nut-free frosting |
Makes 2 (8-inch [20-cm]) cakes and 2 cups (480 ml) frosting

Naturally sweetened only with fruit and sweet potato, this cake still delivers on wow factor. It can be served as is, or you can take things to the next level and assemble a layered celebration cake. The one pictured here features the two cake bases sandwiched together with a generous amount of Fudge Frosting. Brownie Batter Fudge Butter (page 184) is another worthy contender for frosting this moist and craveable cake.

Chocolate Cake

2 cups (350 g) pitted dates, packed

1⅔ cups + 2 tbsp (425 ml) warm water

¾ cup (180 g) mashed, cooked sweet potato, packed

1 tsp apple cider vinegar

2 tsp (10 ml) vanilla extract

1¾ cups (230 g) organic all-purpose flour

¼ cup (36 g) cornstarch or arrowroot powder

⅔ cup (80 g) raw cacao powder or pure unsweetened cocoa powder

1 tsp baking soda

1 tsp baking powder

Fudge Frosting

1 cup (150 g cashews), soaked for at least 4 hours/overnight and drained

1 cup (175 g) pitted medjool dates

¼ cup + 1 tbsp (38 g) raw cacao powder or pure unsweetened cocoa powder

½ tsp pure vanilla powder

Tiny pinch of salt

2 tbsp (30 ml) coconut oil

¼ cup + 1 tbsp (75 ml) water

Preheat the oven to 350°F (180°C) and line two 8-inch (20-cm) springform baking pans with parchment paper.

Add the dates, warm water, sweet potato, vinegar and vanilla to a high-powered blender or food processor and blitz until smooth. *add water slowly or all over*

Add the flour, cornstarch, cacao, baking soda and baking powder to a large mixing bowl and stir to combine. Pour the wet mixture over the dry ingredients and fold until no flour is visible, but do not overmix. If using arrowroot powder, allow this batter to sit for 30 minutes so that the arrowroot has time to hydrate. This will prevent grittiness. If using cornstarch, you can skip the wait time.

Pour the batter into the prepared pans and bake on the center rack of the oven for 30 minutes or until a toothpick inserted in the center of each cake comes out clean.

Remove the cakes from the oven and allow them to cool on baking racks for 10 minutes before carefully releasing them from the tins and allowing them to cool completely.

Prepare the frosting by blitzing the cashews, dates, cacao, vanilla, salt, oil and water in a high-powered blender or food processor until smooth, thick and creamy.

Recipe Note: To make a nut-free layer cake, sandwich the two cake bases together using a layer of Basic Strawberry Chia Jam (page 191) and top with a chocolate topping of your choice such as Easy Avocado Chocolate Whip (page 196), From-Scratch Basic Chocolate Ganache (page 196) or Basic Raw Chocolate in liquid form (page 197).

Lemon & Poppy Seed Cake

Nut- and gluten-free options | Makes 1 (8-inch [20-cm]) cake

The classic flavor pairing of lemon and poppy seed combines with vegan and naturally sweet ingredients to produce sunshine in cake form. It's a delightful tea cake served plain, but to transform this simple, singular cake base into a festive and summery layer cake as pictured, simply bake a couple of these cakes and sandwich them together with a layer of Basic Strawberry Chia Jam (page 191), slather over some Coconut Whip (page 183) or Basic Vanilla Cream Frosting (page 180) and decorate your cake with berries. However you choose to make it, summer will be served!

1¾ cups (230 g) organic all-purpose flour

2½ tsp (12 g) baking powder

1 tbsp (9 g) cornstarch

Pinch of salt

3 tbsp (27 g) coconut sugar

Finely grated lemon zest from 1 to 2 large lemons, depending on taste preference

1½ tbsp (20 g) poppy seeds

⅛ tsp of stevia powder, optional

2 tbsp (30 ml) aquafaba, whisked until lightly frothy and thickened (not whipped)

3–3½ tbsp (45–52 ml) lemon juice (the juice of approximately 1 large lemon)

⅓ cup + 1 tbsp (95 ml) melted coconut oil + a little extra for greasing

¼ cup + 1 tbsp (75 ml) water or oat milk, at room temperature

⅓ cup (80 ml) maple syrup

Toppings and Decorations

1 cup Basic Vanilla Cream Frosting (page 180) mixed with the finely grated zest of ½ a lemon or Coconut Whip (page 183) as pictured here

Fresh or frozen berries

Preheat the oven to 350°F (180°C). Grease an 8-inch (20-cm) springform cake pan and line with parchment paper.

Mix together the flour, baking powder, cornstarch, salt, sugar, zest, poppy seeds and stevia (if using) in a large bowl.

In a medium-size bowl, add the whisked aquafaba, juice, oil, water/oat milk and syrup and whisk thoroughly until smooth. Pour the wet mix over the dry and fold to incorporate, but do not overmix. Pour the batter into the prepared cake pan and bake for 30 minutes or until a toothpick inserted in the center comes out clean. Leave the cake to cool in the pan for 10 minutes, then carefully release the springform mechanism and remove the cake to allow it to cool completely.

Once cooled, the cake can be frosted and decorated, if you like.

Recipe Note: To make the cake gluten-free, replace the organic all-purpose flour with a gluten-free all-purpose flour blend and use water instead of oat milk.

Hummingbird Carrot Bundt Cake

Makes 1 large cake

Think moist and fruity hummingbird cake, traditionally made with banana and pineapple, meets lightly cinnamon-spiced, veggie-packed carrot cake, in a pretty Bundt form. For my third birthday, my mother proudly unveiled a cake with my Cindy doll seemingly baked into the Bundt cake skirt. I burst into tears, while our guests oohed and aahed with delighted amazement. If you make this cake, sans doll, I do hope your guests will be similarly impressed.

---

3 cups (390 g) organic all-purpose flour

½ cup (50 g) unsweetened desiccated coconut, packed

½ cup (75 g) coconut sugar

2 tsp (5 g) ground cinnamon

¼ tsp ground nutmeg

2 tsp (9 g) baking powder

¾ tsp baking soda

½ tsp salt

½ cup (20 g) baby spinach, packed, optional

½ cup + 2 tbsp (150 g) unsweetened applesauce, mashed ripe banana or pumpkin purée

1 tbsp (14 g) chia seeds, finely ground + ¼ cup (60 ml) water

¼ cup (60 ml) aquafaba whisked until slight foamy and thickened (but not whipped)

½ cup (120 ml) olive oil or melted coconut oil + a little extra for greasing

½ cup (120 ml) plant yogurt (oat or soy)

2 tsp vanilla extract

1½ cups (150 g) grated carrots

1 can (8 oz / 227 g) crushed pineapple with juice

¾ cup (80 g) chopped pecans

¾ cup (80 g) chopped walnuts

For Optional Decorations

Basic Vanilla Cream Frosting (page 180) or a double batch of Coconut Whip (page 183)

Slices of dried pineapple

Toasted coconut flakes or sprinkles of choice

Preheat the oven to 325°F (160°C). Grease and lightly flour a Bundt pan. Please do not skip this step, even if you are using non-stick bakeware, because Bundt pans can be tricky when it comes to releasing the cake.

In a large bowl, mix together the flour, coconut, sugar, cinnamon, nutmeg, baking powder, baking soda and salt. If using baby spinach, blitz it together with the applesauce in a small food processor.

In a separate medium-size bowl, mix the chia seeds and water together well. Add the aquafaba, oil, yogurt, applesauce mix and vanilla and mix well. Add the wet ingredients into the dry ingredients. Mix for 3 minutes or until well incorporated. Fold in the carrots, the pineapple and juice and chopped pecans and walnuts.

Pour the batter into the Bundt pan, smooth the surface with the back of a spoon and knock the filled pan against a hard surface to minimize large air bubbles. Bake for 1 hour and 5 minutes. A toothpick inserted in the cake should come out dry if it is done. If it is not, leave the cake in the oven for a further 15 to 20 minutes, but reduce the temperature to 300°F (150°C).

Allow the cake to cool in the pan for 10 minutes, but not longer, and turn it out onto a wire rack to cool completely. Allowing it to cool for at least 2 hours aids in slicing. Frost if desired and decorate with pineapple or sprinkles of choice, such as coconut flakes.

Brownie Batter Babka

Makes 1 loaf

Does a braided bread of rich yeast dough, laced with brownie batter butter, nuts and chocolate make for the perfect lazy weekend baking project? Quite possibly. Make the dough for this on Friday or Saturday evening, and the following day, assemble your surprisingly simple yet impressive looking babka—then treat yourself to a breakfast, brunch or morning tea of champions! This recipe, though not exactly shy on chocolate, contains a quarter of the sweetener found in versions made with processed chocolate spread and thus it is, of course, a treat less sweet. But if moist, delicious, entirely plant-based, home-baked, chocolate-swirled bread appeals to you, your efforts will be rewarded.

Dough

2 cups + 2 tbsp (340 g) organic all-purpose flour, packed and leveled

0.7 oz (20 g) fresh, refrigerated yeast (for sweet dough)

⅓ cup + 1 tsp (85 ml) cashew, oat or almond milk

3 tbsp (27 g) coconut sugar

1 tbsp (14) chia seeds, finely ground + 6 tbsp (90 ml) water

⅓ cup + 1 tbsp (95 ml) olive oil + a little extra for greasing

Pinch of salt

Brownie Batter Filling

⅓ cup (80 ml) Brownie Batter Fudge Butter (page 184)

½ cup (60 g) walnuts, finely chopped

¼ cup (45 g) chopped dark chocolate

Syrup

1½ tbsp (14 g) coconut sugar

2 tbsp (30 ml) freshly boiled water

Day 1

Start by carefully measuring the flour into a medium-size bowl. Use the flat edge of a butter knife to level off the packed cups of flour if measuring without a scale.

In the large bowl of a stand mixer, combine the yeast with the milk. Stir until the yeast dissolves. Add the sugar to the liquid. From the bowl of flour, take ⅓ cup (50 g) of the flour, packed and leveled, and add it to the wet mix. Give the mix a stir to incorporate the flour, then leave it to sit until small bubbles start to appear on the surface, about 10 minutes.

Meanwhile, combine the ground chia seeds and water in a small dish, mixing well to incorporate, then briefly set the mix aside. Using the dough hook on your stand mixer, on a low speed, add the oil to the wet mix, followed by the chia mix and salt. Add the remaining flour, a little at a time, until incorporated. When mixed through, turn up the speed of the mixer to medium-high and knead the dough for 5 minutes until it is smooth, slightly glossy and elastic.

Cover the bowl with a tea towel and refrigerate it overnight.

(continued)

Day 2

Make the Brownie Batter Fudge Butter.

Grease a 9-inch (23-cm) loaf pan with a little olive oil and line it with parchment paper so that the paper overhangs to make for easier babka removal after baking.

Dust a clean work surface with flour and, with a rolling pin, roll the dough out to a rectangular form of about 12 x 18 inches (30 x 45 cm).

Spread the Brownie Batter Fudge Butter evenly over the surface of the dough, ensuring you go all the way to the edge. Sprinkle the chopped walnuts and chocolate over the top.

Beginning from one of the long sides, roll the dough tightly so you end up with a roll that is about 20 inches (50 cm) in length. Using a sharp knife, slice the dough completely in half lengthwise. With the cut sides facing up, overlap the end of one cut half over the other, with the cut sides still facing up. Take the other cut half and fold it over the other.

Continue creating a rope out of the dough by overlapping the 2 halves, ensuring the cut sides are always facing up.

Once complete, carefully lift the loaf and tuck the ends in so that the loaf fits into the prepared loaf pan. Put the loaf pan in the warmest spot in your home and allow it to rise for about 2 hours, until almost doubled in size.

While the dough is rising, prepare the syrup by mixing the coconut sugar with the freshly boiled water in a small dish. Set it aside.

Towards the end of the proofing time, preheat the oven to 390°F (200°C). Bake the babka on the center rack of the oven for 10 minutes, then reduce the heat to 330°F (165°C) and continue to bake it for an additional 15 minutes.

Remove the babka from the oven and spoon the coconut sugar syrup over the top. Allow the babka to cool completely in the pan before carefully removing it. As tempting as it will be to slice the babka while it is warm (I may or may not have tried this), please allow it to cool first to aid in more even slicing.

Recipe Notes: In the case of yeasted bread recipes in particular, I always advocate weighing over measuring with cups if possible, as even small deviations of amounts can adversely affect the finished product.

Leftover babka will keep at room temperature for 3 days, covered, or frozen for up to 3 months, sealed in an airtight container.

Saffron & Marzipan Lucia Scrolls

Makes 35-40 buns

It was imperative that I include a vegan, refined-sugar-free take on the classic Swedish festive treat, lussebullar, in this book. Those with unwavering devotion to pastry convention may well tut at the prospect of a saffron bun with less fat, less sugar, no dairy and no eggs. And yet, I have created these buns precisely because of my love for the comforting, yeast-risen, saffron-infused cheer that my favorite wintertime celebration treat brings.

I find it impossible to discuss the annual celebration of Lucia without reflecting on my first December in Sweden. Unbeknownst to me at the time, I was suffering from the depressive condition known as seasonal affective disorder (the aptly downcast acronym for which is SAD). In the midst of my own Nordic version of *Lost in Translation*, I attended the massive Lucia concert at Stockholm's Globe Arena. Saint Lucia is beloved as the bringer of light during the darkest days of the year—something which initially made little sense to me, having been raised in the warmth of Australian sunshine. Hundreds of school children dressed in white, each holding a candle representing light, lined the aisles of the arena. The lights were dimmed and the children began to sing a melancholy song that wove throughout the arena in rounds. One by one, each child blew out the candle he/she held and stopped singing . . . until only one tiny flickering light remained, from a candle held by a little boy who sang with a trembling yet determined voice all alone in that vast space. The child stopped singing and blew his candle out. Then the lights of the arena sprang on in full force and the crowd burst into applause. And I cried because that beautiful, simple metaphor made sense of it all. I have loved Lucia ever since, and these slightly sweet, marzipan-swirled and sunshiny lussebullar are my own way of honoring the occasion.

Dough

1 cup + 4 tsp (250 ml) oat or cashew milk

1½ cups (350 ml) oat or coconut yogurt

½ cup + 1 tsp (125 ml) olive oil

1.76 oz (50 g) fresh yeast for sweet dough, or 4 tsp (14 g) instant dry yeast

½ cup (75 g) coconut sugar

½ tsp ground saffron

6 cups (950 g) bread flour, packed and leveled

⅓ tsp salt

In a small saucepan over very low heat, add the milk, yogurt and oil, and gently warm the mix to a finger-warm temperature of 95°F (35°C). Pour the liquid mix into the large mixing bowl of a stand mixer and, if using fresh yeast, crumble it into the liquid and stir it in until it dissolves.

Attach the dough hook to the stand mixer. With the mixer on low, add the coconut sugar followed by the saffron, the flour, a cup (160 g) at a time, and the salt to the milk mixture.

If using instant dry yeast, make the liquid mix as above, but omit the yeast. Combine the flour and dry yeast in a large mixing bowl and let it sit for 10 minutes before adding the salt, saffron and sugar. Add the flour mix a tablespoon at a time to the wet mix and mix on low speed to incorporate.

For either yeast, once the flour is mostly incorporated, let the machine work its magic for 5 minutes on medium speed or until the dough can be separated from the sides of the bowl. You can do this process by hand, but it will be a bit of a workout. Allow the dough to rise in the bowl under a clean tea towel for 40 minutes. It should just about double in size.

(continued)

Raw Almond Paste Filling

1½ packed cups (300 g) pitted dates, soaked in boiled water for at least 10 minutes

4 tbsp (60 ml) coconut oil

½ cup (120 ml) lukewarm water

1½ cups (150 g) almond meal

A few drops almond extract (to taste)

To brush

4 tbsp (60 ml) coconut cream, in liquid form

Pinch of coconut sugar, optional

To finish, optional

2 tbsp (30 ml) freshly boiled water

1½ tsp (7 ml) maple syrup

1 tbsp (6 g) coconut sugar

3 tbsp (30 g) chopped blanched almonds, optional

Make the filling by draining the dates and adding them to a food processor with the oil, water, almond meal and almond extract. Blitz well to combine to a smooth, spreadable paste consistency. If it's too thick to spread easily, add an extra tablespoon (15 ml) or so of water.

Line at least 3 trays with a sheet of parchment paper.

Sprinkle a fairly generous amount of flour onto a clean work surface. Tip the dough onto the table and roll it out to a rectangular form 27½ × 19½ inches (70 × 50 cm) in size and about ⅛ inch (2 mm) thick.

Using a silicone spatula, spread the marzipan filling evenly across the dough, right to the edges. Then, beginning from one of the long sides, begin to roll the dough into a log, neatly and tightly. As you roll the dough log it will lengthen somewhat. With a very sharp knife, cut slices ⅔ inch (15 to 20 mm) thick and place them on the baking sheets 12 to 14 buns to a tray, evenly spaced out. You should end up with 35 to 40 buns, depending on the size you cut them.

Proof the buns, allowing them a final rising period of 40 minutes, and then brush them with coconut cream and sprinkle with a pinch of coconut sugar if using. Towards the end of the proofing time, preheat the oven to 435°F (225°C).

Bake the buns one tray at a time on the center rack of the oven, for 7 to 8 minutes or until they are golden brown in color.

If sprinkling with almonds to finish, combine freshly boiled water, syrup and coconut sugar in a small bowl and stir the mixture briskly until the sugar dissolves. Brush a small amount of this syrupy liquid over the still-warm buns, then sprinkle with the chopped almonds.

If making in advance, allow the buns to cool before freezing. They defrost like a dream, by the way!

Blueberry Cupcakes

Nut-free option | Makes 12 cupcakes

With the right balance of sweetness, a light crumb and the delightfully inviting aroma of lemon and blueberry, these cupcakes are sure to be a hit with party guests of all ages. My own little Cupcake (also known as 4-year-old Lillian) is particularly fond of these treats. It may be the case that we unwittingly encouraged her cupcake penchant by giving her the nickname during my pregnancy. Or maybe these cupcakes are just particularly yummy! They do not require frosting, being delicious on their own, but if you're keen to elevate them to party status, I heartily recommend decorating them with perfectly matched Blueberry Lemon Swirl Frosting (page 187) and some fresh blueberries. Don't mention these cupcakes are white sugar–free and vegan—and see if anyone notices!

---

1 tsp apple cider vinegar

¾ cup + 1 tsp (185 ml) cashew or oat milk

2 tbsp cornstarch (18 g) + 2 tbsp (30 ml) water

⅓ cup (50 g) coconut sugar

⅓ cup (80 ml) melted coconut oil

3 tbsp + 1 tsp (50 ml) maple syrup

2 tsp (10 ml) vanilla extract

2 cups (260 g) organic all-purpose flour

1 tsp baking powder

½ tsp baking soda

Pinch of salt

⅓ cup + 4 tsp (10 g) freeze-dried blueberries

Zest of a lemon, finely grated

Blueberry Lemon Swirl Frosting (page 187), for serving

Preheat the oven to 325°F (165°C) convection or 345°F (175°C) non-convection, and line a cupcake tray with paper liners.

Add the vinegar to the milk in a medium-size bowl and allow the mix to sit for 5 minutes. The mix may curdle slightly, but this is a good thing.

In a small bowl, combine the cornstarch and water to create a slurry. Whisk together the milk mixture, sugar, oil, syrup, vanilla and cornstarch slurry in a large mixing bowl.

Sift the flour, baking powder, baking soda and salt into the bowl and fold to incorporate. Add the blueberries and lemon zest and gently fold in. To ensure a lighter cupcake texture, do not overmix.

Fill the cupcake liners two-thirds of the way and bake the cupcakes for 20 to 22 minutes or until baked through. The cupcakes should have a good rise and a toothpick inserted in the middle of a cupcake should come out clean.

Remove the cupcake tray from the oven, transfer the cupcakes to a wire cooling rack and, if decorating, allow them to cool completely first.

Serve them as is or frost with Blueberry Lemon Swirl Frosting.

Any remaining cupcakes can be stored in an airtight container in the freezer for up to 3 months.

Recipe Notes: Fresh blueberries can be used in place of freeze-dried; however, the texture of these cupcakes will not be quite as light.

To make these nut-free, use oat milk.

Lime & Berry Tartlets

Gluten-free | Makes 12 mini tartlets

Zesty lime and juicy berries meet crisp tart shells and cool, creamy filling. These tartlets are easy to assemble, pretty and will make a lovely addition to your summer afternoon tea spread. I've made these treats with the children to celebrate the commencement of Swedish summer holidays and they really are a delightfully simple way to showcase the berry bounty of the warmer months! You can dress them up a little more with optional additions of Coconut Whip and strawberry jam, but fresh berries alone are equally lovely. They may be small and dainty, but these mini tarts pack a zesty punch.

Tart shells

1 cup (90 g) gluten-free rolled oats

¼ cup + 1 tsp (35 g) buckwheat flour

¼ tsp ground cinnamon

2 tbsp (30 ml) maple syrup

Tiny pinch of salt

2 tbsp (30 ml) coconut milk

¼ cup (60 ml) coconut oil

Additional milk or water as needed

Filling

½ lime, zest and juice

1 cup (250 g) oat-based crème fraiche or thick coconut yogurt

2 tbsp (30 ml) maple syrup

Toppings

Berries and/or chopped fruit

¼ cup (60 ml) Basic Strawberry Chia Jam (page 191), optional

⅓ cup (80 ml) Coconut Whip (page 183), optional

Preheat the oven to 350°F (180°C). Lightly grease a mini pie tray.

In a medium-size bowl or a food processor, combine the oats, flour, cinnamon, syrup, salt, milk and oil. If you find the mix too dry, add a teaspoon of water or plant milk at a time to bring the dough together using your hands.

Divide the dough into 12 equal-size portions and press each portion into the prepared tray, forming tartlet shells. They will be somewhat rustic in appearance, but try to make the base and sides approximately the same thickness. Bake the tartlet shells for 8 to 10 minutes or until they are cooked through and lightly browned. Remove the baked tartlet shells from the tray and allow them to cool on a wire rack.

Make the filling by mixing together the zest, juice, crème fraiche and syrup. Spoon enough lime filling into each shell to fill it three-quarters full. Decorate each tartlet with berries, chopped fruit, jam or whip of choice. Serve immediately.

Recipe Note: The dough can be made the day before and stored, covered, in the fridge. The tartlet shells and filling can be made in advance, but once assembled, the tartlets should be decorated and served without too much delay, though keeping them refrigerated for an hour or so shouldn't pose an issue.

Naturally Sweet Vegan Treats

Plum & Marzipan Tarte Tatin

Makes 1 8-serving tarte Tatin

What better way to celebrate stone fruit season than with a sweet and juicy plum tart made from scratch or with accidentally vegan, ready-made pastry, if you are really pressed for time! It may surprise you to know that a food blogger who goes by the pen name Miss Marzipan grew up disliking marzipan. Luckily, I suppose, during my time living in Europe, it has grown on me tremendously. Heck, I even make my own whole-food-based marzipan regularly now. And I'd be totally remiss to not include it here in this vegan version of tarte Tatin, seeing as it turns out that plums and marzipan are perfect partners!

---

1 Olive Oil Short Crust Pastry (page 175)

Raw Marzipan

⅔ cup (115 g) pitted medjool dates, soaked in freshly boiled water for 10 minutes, then drained

⅔ cup (75 g) almond meal

A couple drops of almond extract (to taste)

Tarte Tatin

1 tbsp (9 g) coconut sugar

8–9 ripe large plums, halved and stones removed

For serving, optional

Coconut Whip (page 183), Vanilla Custard (page 161), coconut yogurt or dairy-free ice cream

Make the Olive Oil Short Crust Pastry.

Prepare the marzipan by adding the dates, almond meal and extract to a food processor and blitzing until the mix comes together in a sticky ball of dough. Cover the ball of marzipan and place it in the freezer for 10 minutes or the fridge for at least 30 minutes. If too warm, the marzipan will not roll out successfully. It can be made in advance and kept in the fridge for up to 5 days, stored in an airtight container.

Preheat the oven to 390°F (200°C). Sprinkle the coconut sugar evenly over the base of a 9-inch (23-cm) round cake pan (not springform) or round baking dish.

Arrange the plums cut-side down on top of the coconut sugar. Roll out the marzipan thinly between 2 sheets of parchment paper to a round shape just slightly smaller than the cake pan and place it on top of the plums.

Roll the pastry out to a circle about ¹⁄₁₆ inch (2 mm) thick. Center the pan on the pastry and cut around the pan to make a circle, lay the pastry over the marzipan and tuck the edges of the pastry down around the fruit. Make a small cross in the top of the pastry to let the steam out.

Bake for 20 to 25 minutes, or until the pastry is crisp and golden-brown and the plums are softening, bubbling and cooked through.

Loosen the edges of the tart with a knife, then carefully turn out onto a large plate. Slice and serve it warm with accompaniments of choice.

Recipe Notes: Use ready-made vegan puff pastry instead of Olive Oil Short Crust Pastry for a super quick option.

The recipe works well with canned-in-juice, drained peaches and apricots too.

Our Favorite Gluten-Free Vanilla Caramel Cake

Gluten-free | Makes 1 (8-inch [20-cm]) square cake

Forget the mouth-puckering dryness of the gluten-free bakes of yesteryear, and revel in the delightful texture and caramel notes of our go-to vanilla sponge. This cake is a touch sweeter than some of the other bakes in this book, and I suggest playing around with the amount of coconut sugar to suit your taste and preference. If you decide to cut back on a tablespoon (7 g) of coconut sugar, replace it with a tablespoon (6 g) of almond flour and a pinch (⅛ teaspoon) of stevia powder. This cake is equally lovely served plain or frosted with the Basic Vanilla Cream Frosting (page 180) or Raw Toffee Spread (page 191).

¾ cup (180 ml) almond milk

⅓ cup (80 ml) olive (or melted coconut) oil

¼ cup (60 ml) maple syrup

¼ cup (60 ml) plain unsweetened plant yogurt (soy or coconut-based)

1 tbsp (15 ml) vanilla extract

1 tbsp (15 ml) apple cider vinegar

Couple of drops of almond extract

Pinch of stevia, optional

¾ cup (95 g) buckwheat flour

¾ cup + 1 tbsp (80 g) almond flour

⅓ cup (38 g) coconut sugar

3 tsp (14 g) gluten-free baking powder

Pinch of salt

Preheat the oven to 350°F (180°C). Grease and line an 8 × 8 inch (20 × 20 cm) square baking pan.

Combine the milk, oil, syrup, yogurt, vanilla, vinegar, almond extract and stevia (if using) in a medium-size mixing bowl.

Using a whisk or a fork, mix together the flours, sugar, baking powder and salt in a large mixing bowl. Make a well in the dry ingredients and pour the wet mix into it. Combine the wet mix and dry mix until the batter is smooth.

Pour the batter into the prepared baking pan. Bake for 30 to 35 minutes or until a toothpick inserted in the center of the cake comes out clean.

Please note that your baked cake will be golden brown as opposed to pale golden in color as a result of the combination of flours and sweeteners used. And due to the nature of the flours used in this recipe, this cake does not rise considerably, which gives you a nice even surface that should not dome while baking—a perfect canvas for frosting and decorating, if you so wish.

Recipe Note: To reduce fructose, replace the coconut sugar with ⅓ cup (35 g) extra almond flour and ⅔ teaspoon pure powdered stevia. Replace the maple syrup with organic rice malt syrup.

Naturally Sweet Vegan Treats

Orange & Mango Individual Mini Trifles

Gluten- and alcohol-free | Makes 6 mini trifles

Trifle is one of the first desserts I can recall enjoying as a little girl in London. Fruit, dairy cream, egg custard and sponge cake (often soaked in sherry) form the basis of a classic English trifle. This trifle combines cool and creamy, fruity and spongy, in the pretty layers we all love in a classic trifle. But that, of course, is where the similarities end. The naturally sweetened components of this recipe can be used separately, in conjunction with other treats, or combined, as suggested here, to create a decadent (yet light) and tasty individual trifle.

---

1 Our Favorite Gluten-Free Vanilla Caramel Cake (page 158) or sponge cake of choice

Soft-set Orange & Mango Jelly

¾ cup (120 g) peeled and diced fresh mango (about 1 mango cheek)

1 tbsp (2 g) agar-agar flakes (or 1 tsp agar-agar powder)

1½ cups (360 ml) orange juice

Vanilla Custard

1½ tbsp (13 g) cornstarch + 3 tbsp (45 ml) water

1 cup (240 ml) oat or nut milk

1 cup (240 ml) coconut milk

1 tbsp (9 g) coconut sugar

1 tsp vanilla extract

Pinch of pure vanilla powder

For topping

1 cup (240 ml) Coconut Whip (page 183)

1 tsp orange zest, finely grated

3 tbsp (18 g) desiccated coconut, optional

3 tbsp (20 g) flaked almonds, optional

Make the cake and set it aside to cool.

To make the jelly, tip the mango pieces into a medium-size baking dish or wide pasta bowl.

Add the agar-agar flakes and orange juice to a medium-size saucepan. Bring the mix to a boil and boil for 2½ minutes, stirring continuously. Pour the liquid mix over the mango pieces.

Refrigerate the jelly until it sets. It will not set completely, but will be of a scoopable consistency, much like a thickened purée.

To make the custard, create a slurry by mixing the cornstarch and water in a small bowl. Add the milks to a medium-size saucepan. Add the sugar and bring to bubbling over medium-high heat just below the boiling point, stirring continuously with a wire whisk to allow the coconut sugar to dissolve. Turn the heat down to low-medium. Add the cornstarch mix to the milk mix and allow it to gently simmer, while stirring the custard continuously.

The mix will start to thicken, but if after cooking and stirring for a further 2 minutes, it is not thick enough for your liking, add a further ½ to 1 tablespoons (4 to 9 g) of cornstarch mixed with double the amount of water.

Remove the custard from the heat and add the vanilla extract and powder. If you've developed any visible lumps in the custard as you incorporate the slurry, simply pop a metal sieve over a bowl and strain the custard mix into it. The custard will thicken as it cools. Allow all the components to cool.

To assemble the trifles, simply layer spoonfuls of soft-set jelly, cooled, thickened custard and wedges of cake into individual trifle glasses and top them with whipped coconut cream. Sprinkle with the orange zest or desiccated coconut/ flaked almonds, if using.

Gingerbread Cookies

Grain- and gluten-free | Makes 20-36 cookies

Christmas in Scandinavia would not be the same without the baking and eating of gingerbread cookies, or pepparkakor, as they are known in Sweden. All things deemed to be cozy are employed to infuse our chilly, often snow-dusted Decembers with warmth and festivity. And the Advent period is decidedly cinnamon, allspice, saffron and ginger scented, as a result of ovens across the country working overtime. Pepparkakor are the baked goods most likely to be made with the help of children—who are also known to dress as gingerbread people at this time of year. This easy-to-make recipe produces a crisp, subtly sweet and lightly spiced version of the classic treat. Swedish tradition has it that eating gingerbread cookies will make you kinder. Regardless of whether or not this statement is true, these cookies will certainly add a little low-sugar sweetness to your day. Rolling pins at the ready!

---

1 cup (95 g) almond flour

½ cup (60 g) buckwheat flour + extra for rolling out dough

1 tbsp (9 g) arrowroot flour

¼ tsp baking soda

2 tsp (5 g) ground ginger

1½ tsp (4 g) ground cinnamon

Pinch of ground cloves

Pinch of salt

2 tbsp (15 ml) coconut oil, melted

¼ cup (60 ml) maple syrup

1 tsp–1 tbsp (5–15 ml) water, as needed

For decorating

Coconut flour, for sprinkling, optional

Melted chocolate, optional

Preheat the oven to 350°F (180°C) and line a baking tray with parchment paper.

In a large mixing bowl, combine the flours, baking soda, ginger, cinnamon, cloves and salt. Add the oil and syrup and mix until the dough comes together, adding a touch of water if necessary. If your dough feels particularly tacky/sticky, place it in the fridge for 30 minutes or so to firm up a little, otherwise place it directly on a sheet of parchment paper and dust it with a little buckwheat flour.

Roll the dough out flat with a rolling pin to ¼ inch (6 mm) thickness. Cut out as many gingerbread cookie shapes from the sheet of dough as you can. Re-form, re-dust and re-roll the excess dough to cut out extra cookie shapes.

Arrange the cookies on the prepared baking tray. They won't spread, so they don't require more than a ½-inch (13-mm) space between each other. Bake the cookies for about 6 minutes or until golden and set in the middle.

Once done, remove the cookies from the baking tray and allow them to cool completely on a wire rack before decorating.

Naturally Sweet Vegan Treats

Gingerbread Cake

Nut-free with gluten- and fructose-free options | Makes 1 (9-inch [23-cm]) cake

Gingerbread, in all its forms, is one of the loveliest treats to have on hand during the holidays. This cake is a lighter, less sweet and more delicately spiced version of the classic treat and designed to appeal to even young children, yet the flavors can be dialed up a notch as per your palate and preferences by increasing the amounts of ginger and cinnamon added. It can be served just as it is—and it is lovely on its own—or decorated if you prefer. It's the coziness of Christmas in cake form.

---

1 tbsp (14 g) chia seeds, finely ground + ¼ cup (60 ml) water

½ cup (120 ml) coconut oil, melted + a little extra for greasing the pan

½ cup (120 g) unsweetened applesauce, at room temperature

½ cup (120 ml) maple syrup, at room temperature

2½ cups (325 g) organic all-purpose flour + a little extra for dusting the pan

2½ tbsp (23 g) coconut sugar

2 tsp (9 g) baking powder

2½ tsp (6 g) ground cinnamon

2½ tsp (6 g) ground ginger

1½ tsp (4 g) ground cloves

¼ tsp salt

1 cup (240 ml) hot water

Preheat the oven to 345°F (175°C). Grease and flour a 9-inch (23-cm) square cake pan.

Mix the chia seeds and water briskly in a small bowl using a teaspoon and set it to the side for a minute.

In a medium-size mixing bowl, combine the oil, applesauce and syrup with a wire whisk. Beat in the chia mix and combine well. In a large bowl, sift together the flour, sugar, baking powder, cinnamon, ginger, cloves and salt. Fold in the wet mixture, then stir in the hot water. Pour the batter into the prepared pan.

Bake for 55 minutes or until a toothpick inserted in the center comes out clean. Allow the cake to cool in the pan for at least 20 minutes before removing it, cutting and serving.

Recipe Notes: To make this cake gluten-free, use gluten-free all-purpose flour.

To reduce the fructose in this cake, replace the coconut sugar with ⅛ teaspoon of stevia, replace the applesauce with a ½ cup (120 g) of pumpkin purée and the maple syrup with ½ cup (120 ml) rice malt syrup.

Lingonberry Mince Pies

Alcohol-free | Makes 12 mini mince pies

A new spin on a traditional British Christmas staple with a Scandinavian twist. Growing up in England, and later in Australia, there was perhaps no treat more synonymous with Christmas parties than mince pies. Served hot or cold, they were a deliciously fruity and rich, bite-size addition to every family gathering I can recall. They are largely unknown here in Sweden, and certainly not available ready-made from supermarkets or bakeries. And so, we make our own, adding a local twist in the form of lingonberries. If lingonberries aren't available where you are, swap them for an equivalent amount of cranberries.

Lingonberry Mincemeat

Zest and juice of 1 orange

2 tbsp (30 ml) water

3–4 tbsp (18–36 g) coconut sugar

1 cup (150 g) frozen lingonberries, defrosted (cranberries will work too)

1 tsp ground cinnamon

½ tsp ground allspice

½ tsp ground ginger

¼ cup (55 g) mixed dried fruit (orange peel, raisins, currants)

½ tsp vanilla extract

Maple syrup, to taste, optional

Pastry

1 cup (130 g) organic all-purpose flour

⅓ cup (35 g) almond flour, packed and leveled

6 tbsp (82 g) coconut butter, well mixed

1 tbsp (6 g) coconut sugar

Tiny pinch of salt

1 tbsp (15 ml) aquafaba, whisked until slightly foamy and thickened (not whipped)

3–5 tbsp (45–75 ml) water

To make the mincemeat, grate the orange zest finely. Set the zest to the side. In a small saucepan over medium heat, add the orange juice and water. Dissolve the coconut sugar into the liquid. Add the lingonberries, cinnamon, allspice, ginger, dried fruit and the zest. Bring the mix to a moderate simmer and cook for 10 minutes, stirring gently until the lingonberries have started to burst and the mixture is thick, with only a little liquid remaining.

Remove the pan from the heat and stir in the vanilla. Taste the mincemeat. If it is not sweet enough for your liking, mix in a little maple syrup to taste.

To make the pastry, place the flours, coconut butter, sugar and salt in a food processor. Whizz until combined. Add the aquafaba and then the water a little at a time until the dough starts to come together with a wet crumb texture. To check if the dough will come together properly, pinch it between your fingers. If it is dry and crumbly, add more water and pulse to combine. Using your hands, form the dough into a ball.

Preheat the oven to 400°F (200°C) or 350°F (180°C) for convection baking. Lightly grease a mini pie tray.

Place the pastry on a lightly floured surface. Lay a sheet of parchment paper on top and roll the pastry to a thickness of ⅛ of an inch (3 mm). Cut out circles using a 3-inch (8-cm) cookie/pastry cutter.

Place each pastry round into the prepared tray. Repeat until you have filled the tray. Top each with 2 teaspoons (10 g) of mincemeat. This may sound stingy, but trust me, it bubbles up. Ball up the remaining pastry scraps to roll out, if necessary. Using a star-shaped cookie cutter, cut out 12 small stars (my cookie cutter is 2¼ inches [55 mm] in diameter). Place a star on top of each pie.

(continued)

Naturally Sweet Vegan Treats

Lingonberry Mince Pies (Continued)

Bake the pies for 11 to 14 minutes, or until the pastry is crisp and light golden brown in color. Allow the pies to cool for a few minutes in the tray, and then transfer them to a wire rack until completely cool.

Recipe Notes: If you can't find coconut butter, you may replace it with 3 tablespoons (45 g) of dairy-free spread plus 3 tablespoons (45 g) of non-hydrogenated vegetable shortening.

For pastry recipes, I always advocate weighing over measuring with cups if possible, as even small deviations in amounts can affect the finished product.

Store unused mincemeat in a sterilized, sealed jar for up to a week in the refrigerator or up to 3 months in an airtight container in the freezer.

Store uneaten pies in an airtight container for up to 5 days in the fridge or 3 months in the freezer.

Naturally Sweet Vegan Treats

Orange & Cranberry-Laced Christmas Cake

100% fruit-sweetened, alcohol-free with gluten- and nut-free options | Makes 1 (8-inch [20-cm]) cake

Many believe that a British Christmas celebration isn't complete without a classic Christmas cake on the table. This version departs from convention in a few ways with its lack of sugar, eggs, butter and brandy, but it is no less festive and flavorful. To be very honest, I think I would have much preferred this version when I was a little girl and eating ultra-rich Christmas cake was the common practice at family get-togethers during December! Rich in fruit, dense and delicious, a small slice is enough to satisfy. But at Christmas, I won't hold it against you if you have seconds!

Cake

⅓ cup + 2 tbsp (110 ml) olive oil

¾ cup (150 g) sweet potato purée

1 lemon, finely grated zest and juice only

1 orange, finely grated zest and juice only

1 tbsp (14 g) chia seeds, finely ground + 3 tbsp (45 ml) water

1 cup (120 g) walnuts, chopped

1 cup (150 g) organic dried apricots, chopped

A scant ¾ cup (105 g) soft prunes, chopped

½ cup (75 g) cranberries

½ cup (75 g) raisins

½ cup (75 g) currants

¼ cup + 1 tbsp (50 g) dried orange peel

½ tsp apple cider vinegar

1¼ cups (160 g) organic all-purpose flour (or gluten-free flour blend + 2 tsp [6 g] cornstarch)

1½ tsp (6 g) baking soda

Pinch of salt

1 tsp ground nutmeg

Preheat the oven to 300°F (150°C) convection or 325°F (160°C) non-convection. Grease and line an 8-inch (20-cm) cake pan with parchment paper.

In a large mixing bowl, using a handheld blender (or a fork to whisk briskly), mix together the olive oil, sweet potato purée and lemon and orange zest and juice.

Combine the chia seeds and water in a small bowl. Allow it to sit while you measure the fruit and nuts.

Add the walnuts, apricots, prunes, cranberries, raisins, currants and orange peel to the large mixing bowl with the wet mix. Stir to combine. Add the chia mix and apple cider vinegar to the large bowl, then stir well to incorporate. Using a sieve, sift the flour, baking soda and salt over the mix. Add the nutmeg, cinnamon, ginger, cloves, allspice, a tablespoon or two (15 or 30 ml) of water, as needed, and brandy essence (if using).

Add the mixture to the prepared pan and smooth it over using the back of a large spoon or a silicone spatula.

Bake for 1 hour and 40 minutes or until a toothpick inserted in the center of the cake comes out clean. Remove the cake from the pan and allow it to cool on a wire rack before decorating or serving undecorated.

(continued)

Orange & Cranberry-Laced Christmas Cake (Continued)

2 tsp (5 g) ground cinnamon

1½ tsp (4 g) ground ginger

½ tsp ground cloves

Pinch of ground allspice

1–2 tbsp (15–30 ml) water to bring the mix together

1 tsp brandy flavored essence, optional

Frosting, Optional

1 cup (150 g) cashews, soaked for 4 hours to overnight

1½ tsp (8 ml) vanilla extract

2 tsp (10 ml) maple syrup

2 tsp (10 ml) coconut oil

1 tbsp (15 ml) coconut cream

Toppings and Decorations, Optional

Edible: redcurrants, rosemary sprigs, walnuts, coconut flour

Inedible decor (to be removed before serving): cleaned and sanitized mini pinecones and acorns

To make the optional frosting, drain the cashews and blitz with the vanilla, syrup, oil and cream in a high-powered blender or food processor until smooth, creamy and spreadable. Spread the frosting evenly over the top (or top and sides) of the cake using a spatula. If desired, top the frosted cake with decorations of your choice.

Recipe Notes: To make the cake nut-free, replace the walnuts with ⅓ cup (45 g) pumpkin seeds and ⅓ cup (45 g) sunflower seeds. Instead of frosting, dust lightly with a sprinkle of coconut flour, using a sieve for ease and even distribution.

To make gluten-free, use 1¼ cups (150 g) gluten-free flour with 2 teaspoons (6 g) of cornstarch.

Plant-Based Pastry Pantry

Frostings, sauces, toppings, jams,
homemade plant milk, basic pastry and more

Olive Oil Short Crust Pastry

Nut-free option | Makes 4 to 6 mini crusts for hand pies or one large crust

Four pantry staples plus water, and you're all set! It always pays to have go-to base recipes at hand—especially those that only use pantry staples. It takes a little more effort to make pastry from scratch, of course—but with just four basic ingredients plus water to make this pastry, who's complaining?

1 cup (130 g) organic all-purpose flour

½ cup (60 g) spelt flour

½ cup (50 g) oats, pulsed to a flour in a food processor

¼ tsp salt

⅓ cup + 4 tsp (100 ml) olive oil

¼ cup + 1 tbsp (75 ml) cold water

1 tbsp (15 ml) aquafaba, whisked until lightly frothy (not whipped)

For finishing, optional
A little coconut milk

A small amount of coconut sugar

In a medium-size bowl, add the flours and salt and give them a quick stir with a fork. Pour the oil over the flour and continue to stir with a fork.

When small balls of dough have formed, pour in the cold water and aquafaba. Mash the dough down with the fork to help the liquids incorporate, and bring the dough together in a ball with your hands. Adding a little extra cold water can help bring the dough together, but too much water in a short crust pastry will create tougher dough, and you want to maintain some flakiness.

When rolling out this dough, I recommend two things. First, use 2 sheets of parchment paper to roll it out between instead of flouring the work surface to prevent the dough from becoming overly floured and crumbly. Second, ensure your work surface is clean and a little damp to prevent the parchment paper from sliding as you roll.

To create a golden brown, crispier crust, brush the top of this pastry with coconut milk and sprinkle with a small amount of coconut sugar before baking.

Sweet Gluten-Free Pie Crust

Grain- and gluten-free | Makes 1 (8-inch [20-cm]) pie crust

A crisp and slightly sweet gluten-free pie base, perfect for fillings of your choice.

¾ cup (75 g) almond meal

3 tbsp (21 g) coconut flour

3 tbsp (30) buckwheat flour

1 tbsp (15 ml) aquafaba

1 tbsp (14 g) coconut sugar

1½ tsp (5 g) arrowroot powder, mixed with 1 tsp cold water

1 tsp chia seeds, finely ground, mixed with 1 tbsp (15 ml) cold water

¼ cup (60 ml) coconut oil, melted

½ tsp cinnamon

Tiny pinch of salt

Preheat the oven to 350°F (180°C). Lightly grease an 8-inch (20-cm) round shallow pie pan (with removable base) with coconut oil. Set aside.

Pop the almond meal, flours, aquafaba, sugar, arrowroot mixture, chia mixture, oil, cinnamon and salt into a food processor and process on medium speed until everything combines to form a ball of dough. This should take about 2 minutes. A tiny amount of extra water can be added if needed.

If necessary, pause during the process to scrape down sides of the bowl to ensure everything gets incorporated.

Roll out the dough to a circular shape between two sheets of parchment paper. When the dough is flat and a little larger than 8 inches (20 cm), flip the crust into the pie pan. The dough may break as you flip it into the pan, but just use your fingers to reshape it, pushing it evenly up the sides of the pie pan.

Bake for 18 to 20 minutes or until golden and crisp with the edges just turning golden brown.

Allow the pie crust to cool in the pan for 10 minutes. Gently release the removable bottom of the pan and carefully transfer the crust to a wire rack to cool completely.

Fill the cooled pie crust with a filling of choice. Curd or jam are excellent choices. The Pear & Blackberry Jam with Agar-Agar (page 188) or the Tropical Curd (page 198) work particularly well topped with fruit or berries.

Oat Milk

Nut-free | Makes about 4 cups (1 L)

Oat milk has gained momentous popularity in Sweden in recent years. So threatening was the seemingly overnight fashionability of oat-based alternatives to dairy that one Swedish dairy lobby group famously sued a small local oat milk producer in an attempt to prevent it from using the slogan, "It's like milk, but made for humans." In an ironic twist to the tale, the fuss led to increased publicity for oat milk, which saw its sales go through the roof. What's the oat milk hype about? Try this affordable homemade version of the unsweetened, dairy-free, nut-free milk alternative and see for yourself. Please note: it does taste "oaty."

---

1 cup (90 g) rolled oats

4 cups (960 ml) cold water

Pinch of salt

In a large mixing bowl, combine the oats, water and salt, cover the bowl with a clean tea towel and soak the oats overnight. After soaking, pour the mix into a blender and blitz for at least 2 minutes.

Strain the milk through a nut-milk bag or muslin cloth into a bowl. Pour into a clean, sealable glass jar and keep the oat milk stored in the refrigerator for up to 3 days.

Recipe Note: Always give oat milk a whisk or shake before using.

Cashew Milk

Gluten-free | Makes about 4 cups (1 L)

This is a no-waste, unsweetened, dairy-free milk alternative. As a basic rule of thumb, any nut milk can be made from a ratio of 1 part nuts to 4 parts water. So halving this recipe is just fine if you require a smaller amount of milk. Aside from its versatility and creamy yet neutral flavor, this nut milk can be made thicker and creamier if you so desire, by using a ratio of 1 part nuts to 3 parts water to make 3 cups (720 ml). And another huge benefit of making cashew milk over other varieties? There's no need to strain it post-blending.

---

1 cup (150 g) cashews, soaked in water 4 hours or overnight, drained and rinsed

4 cups (960 ml) water, for blending

Once the cashews have been soaked, drained and rinsed, blitz them with the water in the blender on high speed for 2 to 4 minutes until smooth.

Pour into a clean, sealable glass jar and keep the cashew milk stored in the refrigerator for up to 3 days.

Recipe Note: Always give cashew milk a whisk or shake before using.

Basic Vanilla Cream Frosting

Low-oil and low-sweetener, gluten-free | Makes about 1 cup (240 ml)

Cashew-based buttercream-style frostings are my favorite alternative to vegan frostings containing refined, synthetic imitation butter products and large amounts of icing sugar. First, the inherent creaminess of cashews is a worthy whole-food substitute for dairy and processed dairy alternatives. Second, the subtly sweet neutral flavor profile of this one works well with just about anything and is incredibly customizable—try adding berry powder, crushed cookies or citrus zest. Double the ingredient quantities to make enough frosting to fill and cover a layer cake.

---

1 cup (150 g) cashews, soaked in water 4 hours

2 tsp (10 ml) vanilla extract

2 tsp (10 ml) maple syrup

2 tsp (10 ml) coconut oil

2 tbsp (30 ml) coconut cream

In a food processor, blitz the drained cashews, vanilla, syrup, oil and cream until smooth and creamy. You may need to scrape down the sides of the bowl a couple of times to make sure that everything is incorporated.

Use the frosting to decorate treats of your choice. It holds its shape well.

Coconut Whip

Gluten-, nut- and oil-free with no added unrefined sweetener option | Makes about 1³/₄ cups (415 ml)

Coconut Whip is a staple in our home. As such, I always have a can of coconut milk in the fridge ready to go and several in the pantry awaiting their turn. Versatile, lush and creamy, this whip is the unbeatable whole-food substitute for whipped dairy cream until I find a better alternative. After trial, error and the odd inexplicably seized and curdled batch, I have found that organic, full-fat coconut milk stabilized with guar gum works best, so check the ingredients for the best results. Knowing which brand works means my current-day whips work like a charm. The addition of a small amount of sweetener is optional, and I most often omit it.

1 (14-oz [400 ml]) can organic coconut milk, refrigerated overnight

½ tsp vanilla extract

1 tsp maple syrup, at room temperature, or a pinch of pure stevia powder, optional

Remove the coconut milk can from the fridge, being careful not to flip it over or shake it. Open it and scoop out the solidified layer of coconut cream at the top. Do not include any of the water at the bottom of the can as it will thin out the cream. Reserve the water for adding to oatmeal, smoothies, etc.

Place the cream in a large bowl. Whip the cream for 3 minutes with handheld electric beaters on high speed or until the cream takes on a lighter, fluffy texture with soft peaks resembling lightly whipped cream. Add the vanilla and maple syrup at room temperature to avoid the coconut cream seizing. Whip again for as long as it takes to mix through the additions and reach a desired consistency—5 minutes should be ample.

Use Coconut Whip as a frosting or add it as a topping to puddings, pies and more.

Recipe Notes: It is possible to double the amount and prepare it using a stand mixer with whisk attachment. If using only 1 can of coconut milk, I do not recommend this method, however.

In the unlikely and disappointing event that your coconut cream splits, my recommendation is to pop it into a saucepan over low heat and, stirring, bring the cream back to a liquid state. From here it can be cooled and used to replace plant milk in a nice-cream or baked good recipes, added to coffee as a creamer or drizzled on puddings or porridge like a thin custard. Sadly, nothing solves the problem of splitting, but I can't bear to waste good food, so this is one solution to that particular issue.

Brownie Batter Fudge Butter

Oil- and gluten-free with fructose-free option |
Makes approximately 2 cups (480 ml)

Be warned: this stuff is addictive. And, as the name suggests, you can expect this nut butter to taste like delicious fudgy, chocolate brownie batter. In fact, it's one of the yummiest things I know. To minimize the astringency of the tannin in the walnut skins, a little extra preparation time for soaking is recommended, though you can absolutely skip the first steps if you find yourself in a pinch time-wise or simply don't feel like doing them. The rest of the process is very fast. Indeed, you can make this delicious spread in minutes! Use it on toast, as a cake frosting or filling, in smoothies, on porridge or eat as is! This nut butter will keep for at least 3 days stored in an airtight container in the fridge, although there is every chance it won't last that long once you try it!

---

2 cups (250 g) walnuts

⅓ –½ cup (80–120 ml) almond milk

¼–⅓ cup + 2 tbsp (60–110 ml) maple syrup

4 tbsp (30 g) raw cacao powder or pure unsweetened cocoa powder

1 tsp vanilla extract

Pinch of salt

Soak the walnuts for at least 4 hours to as long as overnight. Then drain them, discard the water and give them a rinse to remove residual tannins.

To prepare the nut butter, blitz the walnuts in a food processor/high-powered blender until they turn to paste. Add the lesser amounts of milk and syrup, adding more if/as needed, and blitz until smooth, blending for about 45 seconds, then scraping down the sides of the food processor bowl with a spatula before blitzing again.

Taste the mix and add a touch more almond milk and/or maple syrup if needed, repeating the blending process until the nut butter has reached a desired consistency. Add in the cacao, vanilla and salt and blitz again. It should be very smooth, but can be thicker or thinner depending upon your preference.

Recipe Notes: For a fructose-free version, use rice malt syrup in place of maple.

For a toastier walnut flavor, after soaking the walnuts for at least 4 hours, drain them and discard the water. Then, toast them on a parchment paper-lined tray at 300°F (150°C) for 10 to 15 minutes to dry them out. Allow the walnuts to cool before using.

 Naturally Sweet Vegan Treats

Blueberry Lemon Swirl Frosting

Gluten-free | Makes about 2 cups (480 ml)

Frosting made from whole foods? Yes. It's a thing. Get the fluff, with none of the guff with this delicious frosting; a more than worthy substitute for one packed with icing sugar, synthetic butter alternatives and artificial food coloring. So pretty. So delicious. And all with less than a teaspoon of added natural sweetener per serving.

---

1 cup (150 g) cashews, soaked in water for 8 hours, then drained

¼ cup (60 ml) coconut oil, melted

¼ cup (60 ml) coconut cream

¼ cup (60 ml) maple syrup

2 tsp (10 ml) vanilla extract

½ tsp freshly squeezed lemon juice

Finely grated zest of half a large lemon

Pinch of salt

¼ cup (7 g) freeze dried blueberries, crushed to a powder (or more for a deeper color)

Add the cashews, oil, cream, syrup, vanilla, juice, zest and salt to a high-powered blender. Blitz until smooth, scraping down the sides of the bowl with a silicone spatula to ensure that everything is incorporated.

Transfer the frosting to a mixing bowl, then place it in the freezer for 20 minutes. Remove the frosting and use an electric handheld whisk to whip until thick, about a minute or two.

Return the mix to the freezer for 15 minutes and then whip again until fluffy. Coconut oil and cream are very temperature-sensitive, so if this frosting is not cold enough, it won't thicken and fluff up to a pipeable consistency and if too cold, it will be granular and "bitty" if you try to pipe it.

Pop half the frosting in a separate bowl and whisk in the crushed blueberries.

Add the blueberry portion of frosting back to the rest of the frosting, and run a spoon through it to create a swirl (without completely blending the two together).

Your two-tone frosting is now ready to be piped or spread onto treats of your choice.

If spreading the frosting, make sure you get a little of the blueberry and a little of the vanilla frosting onto your knife/spoon/spatula. If piping, spoon the frosting into your piping bag, ensuring you include amounts of both the blueberry and the vanilla frosting.

Recipe Notes: Store unused frosting in an airtight container in the fridge for up to 7 days.

The frosting will harden as it chills. If storing in the fridge for later use, allow it to be at room temperature for 20 minutes before using.

Pear & Blackberry Jam with Agar-Agar

Oil-, gluten- and nut-free | Makes 2 cups (480 ml)

Pears and blackberries combine to create this delicate yet flavorful jam that's surprisingly low on natural sweetener. The use of agar-agar in this jam creates a texture that is thick and jelly-like, so if making this jam to spread on toast, try experimenting with the smaller amount of agar-agar. If using it to make the Pear & Blackberry Breakfast Pastries recipe (page 33), I recommend using the larger amount. Regardless, the flavor will be the same, i.e. rather lovely!

---

3 cups (650 g) peeled, diced fresh pear (about 3 pears)

1 cup (140 g) frozen or fresh blackberries

1 tbsp (15 ml) fresh lemon juice

1 tbsp (15 ml) maple syrup

1–1½ tbsp (2–3 g) agar-agar flakes

Place the pears, blackberries, juice and syrup into a large- to medium-size saucepan. Bring the mix to a gentle boil over medium heat for 5 minutes, stirring occasionally.

Add the agar-agar flakes, stirring well to combine. Stir the mix continuously for 3 to 5 minutes. The agar-agar will begin to thicken at the end of the cooking time and will continue to thicken further when cooled.

Remove the saucepan from the heat and allow the mix to cool for 20 minutes, before spooning it into a clean jar. Screw on the lid/s and refrigerate the jam until needed.

Recipe Notes: Note that 1 teaspoon agar-agar powder is equivalent to 1 tablespoon (2 g) of agar-agar flakes.

No agar-agar? Chia seeds can work. The set will differ but the flavor profile will remain the same. Instead of adding agar-agar, after the first 5 minutes of cooking time, add 1 tablespoon (14 g) of finely ground chia seeds mixed with 2 to 3 tablespoons (30 to 45 ml) of water and stir through briskly to incorporate well. Remove the pot from the heat and allow the jam to cool.

Naturally Sweet Vegan Treats

Basic Strawberry Chia Jam

Oil-, gluten- and nut-free | Makes about 1¹/₂ cups (360 ml)

Traditional jams, though arguably delicious and long-lasting, are a markedly sugary affair, with some recipes calling for more sugar than fruit or berry content. To redress the imbalance somewhat and provide an easy alternative to those who want or need one, chia jam has emerged in recent years as a wholesome breakfast-table hero. When we make this version at home, we most often omit the sweetener entirely, but you can add more or less depending on your preference and the level of natural sweetness in the berries you use.

1¾ cups (250 g) frozen or fresh strawberries

A splash of water

1 tbsp (14 g) chia seeds

1–2 tsp (5–10 ml) maple syrup, optional

Squeeze of fresh lemon juice, optional

Pinch of pure vanilla powder, optional

Add the strawberries to a medium-size saucepan. Add a splash of water and, leaving the saucepan lid off, allow the strawberries to gently simmer for 10 minutes or until defrosted and juicy.

Stir in the chia seeds. Add the syrup, lemon juice and vanilla (if using), remove the pan from the heat and allow the jam to cool before storing it in an airtight container. This will keep in the refrigerator for up to 5 days.

*See photo on page 37.

Raw Toffee Spread

Gluten- and nut-free | Makes about 1¹/₄ cups (300 ml)

Spoonable, spreadable and rather delectable, this simple Raw Toffee Spread is one that I have served for years with waffles. In more recent times, I have discovered its aptitude for lusciously topping donuts, cakes, cupcakes and muffins. Quick to whip up, its natural caramel notes and sweetness are a wonderful and easy-to-make enhancement for all manner of treats.

½ cup (90 g) pitted medjool dates

¾ cup (180 ml) warm water

½ tsp vanilla extract

½ tsp ground cinnamon

1 tbsp + 1 tsp (20 ml) coconut oil

½ tsp lemon juice

Pinch of salt to taste

Blitz the dates, water, vanilla, cinnamon, oil, juice and salt until smooth. Add a little extra water if you want a thinner consistency.

Orange Syrup

Gluten- and nut-free with fructose-free option | Makes about ¹/₃ cup (80 ml)

This is a sweet, fragrant, citrus-infused addition to your favorite treats. A little of this syrup goes a long way, and it's particularly lovely served with warm breakfast dishes.

---

3 tbsp (45 ml) maple/rice malt syrup

3 tbsp (45 ml) freshly squeezed orange juice

Pinch of finely grated orange zest (or more to taste)

1 tsp coconut oil

In a small saucepan, combine the syrup, juice and zest. Bring the mix to a gentle simmer, stirring well to incorporate.

Keep the saucepan over low-medium heat for 1 minute, stirring occasionally.

Remove the pan from the heat, stir in the oil and use the syrup warm on pancakes, waffles, cake or puddings.

Recipe Note: To make this fructose-free, use rice malt syrup in place of maple syrup.

Subtly Sweet Caramel Sauce

Gluten-, oil- and nut-free | Makes about ¹/₃ cup (80 ml)

If the previous two recipes are too sweet for your liking, this creamy coconut-based, subtly sweet and caramely sauce might hit the spot!

¾ cup (180 ml) unsweetened coconut cream

2 tbsp (18 g) coconut sugar

Pinch of salt

½ tsp arrowroot powder + 1 tbsp (15 ml) water

1 tsp vanilla extract

Combine the coconut cream, sugar and salt in a small saucepan. Bring the mix to a boil, and then lower the temperature to bring it to a rolling simmer. Stir occasionally.

Around the 5- or 6-minute mark, you may notice a very slight darkening or thickening of the caramel sauce. Even if you don't, it is OK. The slurry will finish the job.

To make the slurry, mix the arrowroot powder and water together in a small dish. Turn the heat off, but leave the saucepan on the stove while you briskly whisk in the slurry to incorporate it well.

Remove the pan from the heat and whisk in the vanilla extract.

The sauce is best served when allowed to cool slightly first.

Naturally Sweet Vegan Treats

Chocolate & Peanut Butter Fudge Topping

Gluten- and oil-free with fructose-free option |
Makes about 1¹/₄ cups (300 ml)

A deliciously satisfying treat topping that can be served in two tasty ways. There is magic in this simple and unassuming topping—and I don't mean on account of the beloved combination of peanut butter and chocolate. Having used this for the longest time as a sauce on pancakes and ice cream, I discovered it could double as a glaze for cupcakes and donuts. What's more, when I set it in the fridge one day, it magically transfigured itself into a creamy spread of chocolaty, peanut butter–spiked gorgeousness (perfect on toast or for spreading over cake as a frosting!).

¾ cup (180 ml) coconut milk

½ cup + 1 tbsp (85 g) chopped dark chocolate

⅓ cup (80 ml) smooth, unsweetened peanut butter

1 tbsp (15 ml) maple/rice malt syrup

Pinch of pure vanilla powder

Pinch of salt, optional

In a small saucepan over low heat, combine the milk, chocolate, peanut butter, syrup, vanilla and salt and allow them to melt together, stirring well to combine. Remove the pan from the heat and use the sauce, warm, straight away. Alternatively, spoon it into a clean jar, allow it to cool and set it in the fridge to become a smooth, creamy chocolate spread to take out at your convenience and spread on your favorite things! It should easily keep for a week.

Recipe Note: To make this fructose-free, use rice malt syrup in place of maple syrup.

Easy Avocado Chocolate Whip

Gluten- and oil-free with fructose- and nut-free options |
Makes about 1 cup (240 ml)

Smooth, rich, velvety and yet surprisingly light, this easy, versatile avocado-based topping comes together in a flash.

---

1 ripe avocado, pitted and peeled

⅓ cup + 1 tbsp (95 ml) plant milk of choice

2 tbsp (30 ml) maple/rice malt syrup (or more or less to taste)

⅓ cup (35 g) raw cacao

1 tsp vanilla extract

Blitz the avocado with the milk, syrup, cacao and vanilla in a small food processor until well combined and smooth. Use as a topping for nice-cream or pudding, add to oatmeal and more!

Recipe Note: To make this fructose-free, use rice malt syrup in place of maple syrup.

From-Scratch Basic Chocolate Ganache

Gluten- and nut-free with fructose-free option |
Makes about ²/₃ cup (160 ml)

This ganache makes good use of pantry items when dark chocolate is not on hand. Shiny and delicious, it's perfect for jazzing up semi-sweet treats.

⅓ cup + 4 tsp (100 ml) maple/rice malt syrup (or more or less to taste)

3 tbsp (45 ml) coconut oil, melted

⅓ cup (35 g) cacao + more to achieve desired consistency, if needed

In a small saucepan over low heat, add the syrup, oil and cacao, stirring until smooth and well combined.

Remove the pan from the heat and use the ganache warm on pancakes, waffles, cake or puddings.

Recipe Note: To make this fructose-free, use rice malt syrup in place of maple syrup.

*See photo on page 127.

Naturally Sweet Vegan Treats

Basic Raw Chocolate

Gluten- and nut-free with fructose-free option |
Makes about 1 cup (240 ml) chocolate mix

One of the most basic staples of the aspiring plant-based pastry maker's repertoire, raw chocolate is a cinch to make and very versatile. In its liquid form it can be used as a topping or to decorate cakes. This version is a low-key, 3-ingredient little ripper*. (*Aussie slang which indicates something is good!)

---

1 cup (85 g) raw cacao powder

½ cup (120 ml) coconut oil, melted

¼ cup (60 ml) maple/rice malt syrup

Add the cacao, oil and syrup to a medium-size mixing bowl and mix until well combined and smooth.

To set it, pour/spoon the mix into silicone molds or ice cube trays and pop in the fridge or freezer until completely set. The time will vary according to the size of the molds used, but wait at least 25 minutes before checking the status of your chocolate. Eat the chocolate as it is or use the shapes to decorate other treats.

This chocolate can also be made in bark form. Line a brownie pan with parchment paper, pour/spoon in the chocolate mix, then sprinkle with 2 to 4 tablespoons of dried berries, nuts or seeds of choice and set the pan in the fridge or freezer until the chocolate is completely set. Once set, cut it into shards. Eat as it is or use the shards to decorate other treats.

Recipe Note: To make this fructose-free, use rice malt syrup in place of maple syrup.

*See photo on page 128.

Tropical Curd

Grain-, oil- and gluten-free with no added natural sweetener option | Makes about 1¹/₂ cups (360 ml)

Fruit curd with no white sugar, no eggs and no butter? Not only is it possible, it's delicious! One and a half cups (287 g)—yes, cups—of white sugar is common in many a curd recipe—including my former favorite lemon curd from the past. This recipe, in contrast, features the delightful fruity flavor burst you would want from any curd, with a ludicrously little 1 tablespoon (15 ml) of added natural sweetener in the form of maple syrup. The addition of passion fruit is non-negotiable; it truly elevates the flavor of this yummy, soft-set Tropical Curd. There are several things I really miss about Australia now that I have lived in Scandinavia for 13 years. Loved ones who live there, of course, and the warm sunshine, white sand beaches (oh, the beaches!) and Aussie-grown tropical fruit count among them. No matter the weather where you are, make this curd and find yourself temporarily transported somewhere warm and balmy. It does the trick for me, in any case! Use this curd in pies or cakes, or as a topping for puddings, ice-cream, oatmeal and more.

1½ tbsp (14 g) arrowroot powder + 3 tbsp (45 ml) water

1 tbsp (15 ml) lemon juice (from half a lemon)

1 tbsp (15 ml) lime juice (from 1 lime)

1½ cups (325 g) peeled, pitted and roughly chopped mango, about 2 medium-size mangoes

1 tbsp (15 ml) maple syrup

2 tbsp (30 ml) coconut milk

Pulp from 1 to 2 passion fruits

In a small bowl, combine the arrowroot powder, water, and lemon and lime juices to make a slurry. Set this bowl aside while you prepare the mango purée.

Purée the mango in a food processor or blender until smooth. Use a sieve and silicone spatula to strain the mix into a small- to medium-size saucepan. Dispose of any stringy bits remaining in the sieve.

Over medium heat, cook the mango purée until bubbling, stirring frequently. Add the maple syrup and stir thoroughly. Whisk the purée mix constantly as you add the arrowroot slurry. The curd should start to thicken.

After a minute or two, remove the saucepan from the heat. Taste the curd and add a little extra lime/lemon juice if desired.

Stir in the coconut milk and passion fruit pulp. Allow the curd to cool before using.

Recipe Notes: Do make sure your mangoes are nice and ripe as their natural sweetness will contribute to the flavor.

If you're keen to try this curd completely sweetener-free, simply omit the maple syrup and, once made, taste the curd to ensure it's to your liking. You can always stir a little natural sweetener through it post-making.

Remaining curd can be stored in a sterilized, sealed jar in the fridge for up to 3 days after making.

Naturally Sweet Vegan Treats

Maple-Glazed Dehydrated Citrus Slices

Oil-, gluten- and nut-free | Makes at least 12 citrus slices

Who doesn't love naturally pretty cake decor? This simple recipe does not produce candied citrus slices, as it's made using less than 2 teaspoons (10 ml) of maple syrup, whereas candied citrus slices are typically made with around 2 cups (384 g) of refined sugar. They are, however, equally pretty and make appealing decorations for your cakes and treats.

---

1 lemon

1 navel or blood orange

1½ tsp (7 ml) maple syrup, optional

Preheat the oven to 185°F (85°C). Line a baking tray with parchment paper or silicone baking mat.

Slice the lemon and orange across the grain to make round wheels as thin as possible without tearing. Arrange the fruit slices on the prepared tray without overlapping. Use a pastry brush to lightly brush each slice including the peel with maple syrup, if using.

Place the tray in the oven and bake the slices until the peels have dried and the flesh has turned translucent, 2 to 2½ hours. Once cooled and completely dried, the slices can be used immediately to decorate treats or placed in an airtight container and kept in the fridge for up to a week, and the freezer for up to 3 months.

Unicorn Sprinkles

Oil-, gluten-, unrefined sweetener-, artificial food coloring- and nut-free | Makes ¹/₃ cup (20 g) single-colored sprinkles

Variations of colored coconut sprinkles can be found all over Pinterest and the blogosphere. Given that this is the quickest way I've found to prepare them, and that children seem to be universally delighted by the prettiness of sprinkles, I'd be remiss not to share my interpretation here. Keeping these Unicorn Sprinkles naturally enchanting, I chose not to add any sweetener, allowing the inherent sweetness of the coconut to do its thing. Pick your favorite color below and go make some magic.

---

¹/₃ cup (20 g) unsweetened desiccated coconut

Green Sprinkles
1 tbsp (15 ml) juice from 2½ oz (70 g) defrosted frozen spinach, puréed then strained

Pink Sprinkles
1 tbsp (15 ml) beet juice

Yellow Sprinkles
1 tsp ground turmeric mixed with 1 tbsp (15 ml) warm water

Purple Sprinkles
1 tbsp (15 ml) strained juice from puréed defrosted frozen blueberries

Preheat the oven to 220°F (105°C) and line a baking tray with parchment paper.

In a mixing bowl, add the coconut and the coloring agent of your choice. Mix well with a spoon to combine.

Pour the colored coconut onto the prepared tray, spread it out to allow for more even drying and place it in the oven. Allow the mix to dry for 20 minutes.

Give the coconut a stir and reduce the oven temperature to 210°F (100°C), allowing it to dry for a further 10 minutes.

Give the coconut another stir and turn off the oven. If needed allow the tray to sit in the oven so that the residual heat can finish the drying process. Once cooled and completely dried, the coconut can be used immediately to decorate treats or placed in a small, clean jar and kept in the fridge for up to a week, and the freezer for up to 3 months.

Recipe Note: For the green sprinkles you can replace the spinach juice with 1 teaspoon matcha mixed with 1 tablespoon (15 ml) of water.

Acknowledgments

It's important for me to acknowledge where I come from. Firstly, not a single page of this book would have been possible without my family's unwavering support (I love you). And, it's no doubt apt to thank the people who somehow discovered my anonymous blog and started following it back in 2011. There were 7 of you. If you're reading this, you know who you are, and I am still humbled! I'd also like to thank all those who have supported me on Instagram because, without doubt, my life would look very different if it wasn't for you! Likewise, had I not discovered the work of Sarah Wilson and Poh Ling Yeow, and had support from both of these truly amazing, inspirational women, you would definitely not be reading these words right now. They have had a huge impact on my life in every way and I am incredibly grateful to Robin Eley (who has been my biggest life-long inspiration) for introducing me to Poh in 2014, thus inadvertently changing the course of my life.

Thanks also to Malin Randeniye, ultra-talented Swedish food entrepreneur and clinical dietician, who has supported and encouraged me since we randomly connected in 2015; to boss babe of Melbourne, Sarah Holloway, whose advice has been invaluable; Diana Tencic, renowned food/fitness coach and confidante (who also tested recipes for this book); project manager extraordinaire, Ulrica Kretz, for championing me since 2008; gifted naturopath, Julia Michelle, for her support and timely advice; my friends in recovery; my fellow Institute for Integrative Nutrition grads; my I Quit Sugar friends; the amazing feedfeed team (particularly Julie) for all their support over the years; the entire, wonderful Instagram foodie community (I can't possibly name you all, but I hope you know I'm genuinely thankful for you); and to my friends and relatives who may or may not have an interest in vegan/sugar-free food, blogging or what have you, and yet stick around, occasionally putting up with their meals getting cold on lunch dates so I can shoot them first (I am working on that!).

I am very grateful for the inspiration and encouragement I have received from talented food and photography professionals, the amazing Rachel Khoo, Ditte Ingemann, Béatrice Peltre, Simone van den Berg, Nik Märak and Maximillian Lundin, Sweden's most renowned vegan chef and one of Europe's foremost plant-based food revolutionaries, among them. Thank you to the magazines and brands that have offered me opportunities and to my former colleagues for continuing to encourage me.

And thank you for picking up this book!

Working as a creative professional over many years, I have had to learn how to take constructive criticism on the chin. However, as part of a corporate creative team, I've had the buffer of a certain level of anonymity to help cope with my anxiousness around that stuff. As this is my first solo published work, and one with my name on it, the desire to represent my passion adequately has

Naturally Sweet Vegan Treats

been amplified tenfold. Luckily, I have had support from my ever-steadfast rock of a husband who tries my new creations without question or pause, my endlessly positive children and my friends, family and social media connections near and far.

I must thank my loyal and dedicated recipe testers and review crew; the most amazing mix of food bloggers, sugar quitters, vegans, omnivores, professional chefs, self-proclaimed newbie bakers, passionate home cooks and their parents/children/friends. I am so touched and so grateful for your support. Thank you especially Libbi Coldicott, Roberta Dall'Alba, Aileen Libbey, chef Miklós Somogyvári, Ellen Termine, Lisa Reid, Lilli Eley, Rachel Eley, Karen Plummer, Leo Plummer, Mira Lindgren, Tara Grosboll, Rani Hansen, Catherine McCormick, Ella Dahl, Natalie Beran, Elenor Jean, Amanda Radomi, Kristina Starborg, Mary Crout, Brenda Eldridge, naturopath Angelica Hazel Toutounji, Rebecca Choate, Odile Joly-Petit, Sarah Hopkins, Jessica Razzoli, chef Jojje Tillberg, Jessica Hilwëyn, Tony Hilwëyn, Windla Hilwëyn, Linda Trujillo, Kim Hudson, Kari Pahlman, Claire Mitchell and the incredible Nele Franke and Sue Kirkland for their enthusiastic and invaluable eleventh hour support.

Many thanks also to Dr. Jennifer Protudjer at the Centre for Occupational and Environmental Medicine at Karolinska Institutet in Stockholm, Sweden, for reviewing the outline and recipes for this book, and even testing some herself!

Thank you to Page Street Publishing (particularly my editor, Marissa G.) for finding me, having faith in me and investing so much trust in me. I'm grateful, humbled, overwhelmed and, even as I type these words, still wading through occasional waves of disbelief. Just months ago, I walked into a scheduled meeting with my manager and found myself resigning from a good corporate job (one that I loved) because I finally felt compelled to take the risk of working for myself.

The timing seemed incredibly wrong in some ways (three small children, new home, bigger mortgage, etc.), but somehow felt right. My manager asked me what my plans were. I was honest and said I had nothing concrete lined up, but that I had to follow my heart, adding that I felt the need to engage with one career path or project wholeheartedly, as opposed to two (or more) halfheartedly. I wanted to leave before that happened. And I wanted to leave on a good note.

And so, I left the office building that day buzzing with nervousness and excitement, feeling a little lost and disoriented. Literally four hours later I was on a conference call with Page Street Publishing, and I was offered the opportunity to put this book together.

About the Author

Marisa is a professional corporate art director, recipe developer and food photographer turned WAHM (Work at Home Mum), with a particular passion for plant-based food and baking. She started her blog, Miss Marzipan, in 2011 after her first pregnancy and, despite remaining anonymous on her online channels for 3 years, continued to share content and managed to attract a supportive social media following, for which she is incredibly grateful.

Born in London and raised in Australia, Marisa now lives with her vegan husband and 3 young children in central Stockholm, Sweden. Marisa's children are her kitchen helpers. They love to go grocery shopping with her and are proud of the fact that they know their avocados from their aubergines.

Marisa's perfect day would involve sunshine, some form of physical activity, reflection/meditation, indulging in creative pursuits, cooking (or at the very least, eating!) and cuddles. And if it all took place in an exotic location of some description, she wouldn't complain.

Index

Naturally Sweet Vegan Treats

Naturally Sweet Vegan Treats